Sacred Texts
of the
World's Religions

Compiled by

Mark R. Woodward

PEARSON

Prentice
Hall

Upper Saddle River, NJ 07458

© 2004 by PEARSON EDUCATION, INC.
Upper Saddle River, New Jersey 07458

ISBN 0-13-049522-0

Printed in the United States of America

Contents

Indigenous Sacred Ways   1

      Songs play an important role in Navajo and other Native American religions. This text concerns the origins of Navajo songs. It is followed by translations.

      The Yoruba are among the indigenous peoples of West Africa. Many Yoruba were brought to the Americas as slaves. Their beliefs, rituals, and folklore have greatly influenced the development of African American religious traditions, especially in the Caribbean, Central, and South America. There is currently a revival of interest in Yoruba religion and culture among U.S. African Americans.

✸ *Hinduism* *21*

 *Jainism*   *34*

❀ *Buddhism*   **40**

❀ *Taoism and Confucianism*   **67**

✿ *Christianity*   *98*

✿ *Islam*   *115*

✹ *Sikhism* 131

✹ *New Religious Movements* 134

Religion continues to grow and expand. Some traditions, including many of the indigenous traditions of the Americas and Africa, have declined precipitously in the last century. Many appear to be headed for extinction. During this same period many new religions developed. Some of these are directly related to older, more established religions. Others, especially "New Age" faiths, are eclectic, drawing on aspects of several historical traditions and fresh religious insights. There are so many new religions that it is not possible to include all of them in an anthology of this length. I have selected two.

The Bahai faith is an example of a new religion that has deep roots in a "parent" religion—Islam. Of the world's "new religious movements" the Bahai faith is among the most widely distributed. Missionaries have carried the faith to most of the countries of the world. Perhaps the most striking examples of conversion to Bahai are among the native peoples of South America.

Beliefs and traditions concerning the Vortex Experience of Sedona, Arizona are examples of New Age Spirituality. The text included here draws on Native American, South Asian, and Chinese traditions.

Preface

The texts included in this reader were selected to augment the discussions of the world's major religions in Mary Pat Fisher's textbook *Living Religions*. The chapter structure mirrors that of the textbook. There are chapters for Indigenous Religions, Hinduism, Jainism, Buddhism, Taoism and Confucianism, Shinto, Judaism, Christianity, Islam, Sikhism, and New Religious Movements. The texts have been selected to reflect both the core themes and diversity of each of these religious traditions.

Mark R. Woodward
Associate Professor
Department of Religious Studies
Arizona State University

Credits

2.1 A Cherokee Origin Tale, from J. Mooney. *Myths of the Cherokee. 19th Annual Report of the Bureau of Ethnology*, Part 1 Washington, DC 1897-1898.

2.2 A Tale of Kinnaekai, from Washington Mathews; Foreword by John Farella; Orthographic Note by Robert Young. *The Night Chant, A Navajo Ceremony*, Salt Lake City: University of Utah Press 1995. Originally published: New York Knickerbocker Press, 1902

2.3 A Navajo Song from Washington Mathews; Foreword by John Farella; Orthographic Note by Robert Young. *The Night Chant, A Navajo Ceremony*, Salt Lake City: University of Utah Press 1995. Originally published: New York Knickerbocker Press, 1902

2.41 A Yoruba Origin Tale, From Fashina Felade, http://www.anet.net/~ifa/index.html

2.42 The Yoruba Circle of Life, From Fashina Felade, http://www.anet.net/~ifa/index.html

2.43 A Yoruba Morning Prayer, From Fashina Felade, http://www.anet.net/~ifa/index.html

2.5 A Maori Origin Tale, http://www.sacred-texts.com/pac/mrm/mrm04.htm

2.6 Indigenous Sacred Ways in the Modern World: A Conversation between Native American and Maori Spiritual Leaders, From http://www.crystalinks.com/macki.htm

3.11 Invocation of Angi, *The RIG VEDA* Ralph T.H. Griffith, translator, 1889, http://www.sacred-texts.com/hin/rigveda/rv10129.htm

3.12 The Sacrifice of Purusha, *The RIG VEDA* Ralph T.H. Griffith, translator, 1889, http://www.sacred-texts.com/hin/rigveda/rv10129.htm

3.13 An Origin Tale From the Rig Veda, *The RIG VEDA* Ralph T.H. Griffith, translator, 1889, http://www.sacred-texts.com/hin/rigveda/rv10129.htm

3.2 Max Müllers' translation of the Upanishads, Volume Two. (1884) (Volume 15 of the Sacred Books of the East.) http://www.hinduwebsite.com/sacredscripts/brihad_max1.htm

3.3   The Laws of Manu and the Stages of Life. *The Laws of Manu,* George Bühler, translator *(Sacred Books of the East, Volume 25)* http://www.sacred-texts.com/hin/manu.htm

3.4   Selections from the Bhagavadita, *The Bhagavad-Gita* by Dr. Ramanada Prasad http://www.gita4free.com/english_completegita.html

4.1   Kastur Lalwani, Translator, *The Kapla Sutra of Bhadrabahu Swami* LIVES OF THE GINAS. LIFE OF MAHAVIRA. http://www.sacred-texts.com/jai/kalpa.htm

4.2   Ankaranga Sutra: Begging for Food, from Hermann Jacobi, translator, *Jaina Sutras Part I the Akaranga Sutra The Kapla Sutra* http://www.sacred-texts.com/jai/akaranga.htm

5.11   Selections from *The Dhammapada.* From Henry Warren, *Buddhism in Translation,* Cambridge: Harvard University Press 1906.

5.12   Selections from *The Discourse on the Analysis of the Undefiled,* From I. Homoer, *The Collection of The Middle Length Sayings* (Majjhima Nikaya) Volume III *The Final Fifty Discourses* (Uparipannasa) Oxford, The Pali Text Society, 1996

5.13   A Thai Buddhist Sermon Konrad Kingshill, Compiler/Editor, "Of Mechanical Swans and Rain-Producing Elephants: A Collection of Thai and Lanna Thai Tales and Sermons." Tempe: Arizona State University, Program for Southeast Asian Studies, Monograph Series Press, 2000.

5.21   The Vajracchedika Prajna paramita Sutra http://www.buddhistinformation.com/diamondsutra.htm

5.22   Wonderful Voice Bodhisattva. Summary of *The Sutra of the Lotus Flower of The Wonderful Dharma Dharma Wheel* http://www.ibc-rk.org/chapter%2024.htm

5.23   *Hymn to Perfect Wisdom,* Osel Shen Phen Ling Tibetan Buddhist Center http://www.fpmt-osel.org/meditate/hrtsutra.htm

5.24   Buddhist Texts from China and Japan. From the Buddhist Association of the United States, http://www.sinc.sunysb.edu/Clubs/buddhism/huineng/huineng10.html

6.11   *On Tolerance.* From the Buddhist Association of the United States http://www.clas.ufl.edu/users/gthursby/taoism/cz-text2.htm#ON

6.12   Selections from the Tao-te Ching. Written by Lao-Tzu *The Way of Dharma and It's Power A New Translation For the Public Domain* by J. H. McDonald http://www.geocities.com/shoshindojo

6.21   Selections from the *Analects of Confucius,* Arthur Whaely, translator, *The Analects of Confucius,* New York, Vintage, 1938.

6.22   The Meaning and Value of Rituals, Y. Mei translator, *Sources if Chinese Tradition,* William de Bary editor, New York: Columbia University

7.1   *The Kojiki,* B.H. Chamberlain, translator 1882, Part I.- The Birth of the Deities. The Beginning of Heaven And Earth. http://www.sacred-texts.com/shi/kojiki.htm

8.1   Selections from the bible. Scripture quotations are from the *New Revised Standard Version of the Bible,* copyright (c) 1989 by the Division of Christian Education of the National Council of the Churches of Christ in the USA. Used by permission. All rights reserved.

8.11   A Biblical Origin Tale

8.12   Abraham, The Father of Many Nations

8.13   Exodus, the Scriptural Warrant for Pasover

8   8.14   Law and Ethics

8.15   Absolute Monotheism

8.21   Selections from the Talmund Babylonian Talmud, translated by Michael L.. Rodkinson, Book 5 (Vols. IX and X) [1918] Tracts Aboth, Derech Eretz-Rabba, Eretz-Zuta, and Baba Kama (First Gate) http://www.sacred-texts.com/jud/t05/abo05.htm

8.22   Selections from the *Midrash.* From John Townsend, Translator, Translated to English with Introduction Indices and Brief Notes. Volume I Genesis Hoboken KTAV Publishing House, 1998.

8.23   Selections from the *Mishnah,* from Lawrence Schiffman, Texts and Traditions. A Source Reader for the Study of Second Temple Rabbinic Judaism. Volume I Genesis Hoboken KTAV Publishing House, 1998.

8.24   Selections from *Halakhah,* an Encyclopaedia of the Law of Judaism: Vol. 1, PT. 4: Inside the Walls of the Israelite Household, PT. A. Leiden: Brill Academic Publishers, 2000.

8.3   A 16th Century Jewish Sermon, from Marc Saperstein, *Jewish Preaching 1200-1800 An Anthology,* Yale University Press, 1989.

9.1   Selections from the New Testament Scripture. Quotations are from the *New Revised Standard Version of the Bible,* copyright (c) 1989 by the Division of Christian Education of the National Council of the Churches of Christ in the USA. Used by permission. All rights reserved.

9.11   John the Baptist

9.12   The Sermon on the Mount

9.13   The Crucifixion and Ressurection

9.2   Selections from *The Confessions and Letters of St. Augustin, with a Sketch of his Life and Work* Creator(s): Schaff, Philip (1819-1893) Print Basis: New York: Christian Literature Publishing Co., 1886 http://www.ccel.org/ccel/schaff/npnf101.txt

9.3 Selections from the *Rule of St. Benedict*, From Leonard Doyle, Translator, *SaintBenedicts Rule for Monasteries, The Order of St. Benedict.* www.osb.org/rb/text/rbejms1.html

9.4 "To the Bishops of Sradinia." Selections from a letter from Pope Clemet XIV, from Claudia Carlen, *The Papal Encyclicals 1740-1878*

9.5 Martin Luther's Ninety Five Theses, from Timothy Lull, Editor, *Martin Luther's Basic Theological Writings*, Minneapolis, Fortress Press, 1989

10.1 Selections from the Qur'an. An electronic version of The Holy Qur'an, translated by M.H. Shakir and published by Tahrike Tarsile Qur'an, Inc

10.11 The Opening

10.12 Abraham

10.13 Al-Hijr

10.14 Light

10.3 The Alchemy of Happiness, 1909 By Al Ghazzali Claud Field, translator, b. 1863, d. 1941. http://www.sacred-texts.com/isl/tah/tah05.htm

10.4 Selections from the Mystical Poetry of Rumi, From Andrew Harvey, Translator, *The Teachings of Rumi*, Boston, Shambala, 1999.

11.1 Selections from Shri Guru Granth Sahib http://www.sacred-texts.com/skh/granth/gr01.htm

12.1 Selections from the Kitab-I-Aqadas, http://www.sacred-texts.com/bhi/aqdas.htm

12.2 Selections from the Sedona Vortex Experience. From Gaia Lamb and Shinan Barclay, *The Secona Vortex Experience*, Sedona: Sunlight Productions, 1987

Indiginous Sacred Ways

2.1   A Cherokee Origin Tale

The earth is a great island floating in a sea of water, and suspended at each of the four cardinal points by a cord hanging down from the sky vault, which is of solid rock. When the world grows old and worn out, the people will die and the cords will break and let the earth sink down into the ocean, and all will be water again. The Indians are afraid of this.

When all was water, the animals were above in Galun'lati, beyond the arch; but it was very much crowded, and they were wanting more room. They wondered what was below the water, and at last Dayuni'si, "Beaver's Grandchild," the little Water-beetle, offered to go and see if it could learn. It darted in every direction over the surface of the water, but could find no firm place to rest. Then it dived to the bottom and came up with some soft mud, which began to grow and spread on every side until it became the island which we call the earth. It was afterward fastened to the sky with four cords, but no one remembers who did this.

At first the earth was flat and very soft and wet. The animals were anxious to get down, and sent out different birds to see if it was yet dry, but they found no place to alight and came back again to Galun'lati. At last it seemed to be time, and they sent out the Buzzard and told him to go and make ready for them. This was the Great Buzzard, the father of all the buzzards we see now. He flew all over the earth, low down near the ground, and it was still soft. When he reached the Cherokee country, he was very tired, and his wings began to flap and strike the ground, and wherever they struck the earth there was a valley, and where they turned up again there was a mountain. When the animals above saw this, they were afraid that the whole world would be mountains, so they called him back, but the Cherokee country remains full of mountains to this day.

When the earth was dry and the animals came down, it was still dark, so they got the sun and set it in a track to go every day across the island from east to west,

1

just overhead. It was too hot this way, and Tsiska'gili, the Red Crawfish had his shell scorched a bright red, so that his meat was spoiled; and the Cherokee do not eat it. The conjurers put the sun another hand-breadth higher in the air, but it was still too hot. They raised it another time, and another, until it was seven handbreadths high and just under the sky arch. Then it was right, and they left it so. This is why the conjurers call the highest place Gulkwa'gine Di'galun'latiyun, "the seventh height," because it is seven hand-breadths above the earth. Every day the sun goes along under this arch, and returns at night on the upper side to the starting place.

There is another world under this, and it is like ours in everything-animals, plants, and people-save that the seasons are different. The streams that come down from the mountains are the trails by which we reach this underworld, and the springs at their heads are the doorways by which we enter it, but to do this one must fast and go to water and have one of the underground people for a guide. We know that the seasons in the underworld are different from ours, because the water in the springs is always warmer in winter and cooler in summer than the outer air.

When the animals and plants were first made-we do not know by whom-they were told to watch and keep awake for seven nights, just as young men now fast and keep awake when they pray to their medicine. They tried to do this, and nearly all were awake through the first night, but the next night several dropped off to sleep, and the third night others were asleep, and then others, until, on the seventh night, of all the animals only the owl, the panther, and one or two more were still awake. To these were given the power to see and to go about in the dark, and to make prey of the birds and animals which must sleep at night. Of the trees only the cedar, the pine, the spruce, the holly, and the laurel were awake to the end, and to them it was given to be always green and to be greatest for medicine, but to the others it was said: "Because you have not endured to the end you shall lose your hair every winter."

Men came after the animals and plants. At first there were only a brother and sister until he struck her with a fish and told her to multiply, and so it was. In seven days a child was born to her, and thereafter every seven days another, and they increased very fast until there was danger that the world could not keep them. Then it was made that a woman should have only one child in a year, and it has been so ever since.

2.2   A Tale of Kininaékai

In the ancient days, there were four songs which you had to sing if you would enter the White House The first was sung when you were ascending the cliff; the second, when you entered the first doorway; the third, when you walked around inside the house; and the fourth, when you were prepared to leave. You climbed up from the ground to the house on a rainbow. All this was in the old days. You cannot climb that way now. In those days, *Hayolkál Askí*, Dawn Boy, went there on a rainbow.

In the ancient days, there lived in this house a chief of the house. There were four rooms and four doors, and there were sentinels at each door. At the first door there were two big lightnings, one on each side; at the second door there were two bears; at the third door there were two red-headed snakes, which could charm you from afar, before you got near them; and at the fourth door there were two rattlesnakes.

Of course few people ever visited the place, for if the visitor were not a holy one some of these sentinels would surely kill him. They were vigilant. The chief of the house and his subordinates had these songs, by the power of which they could enter and quiet the sentinels, who always showed signs of anger when any one approached them.

Dawn Boy got leave from *Hastséyalti* to go to White House. *Hastséyalti* instructed him how to get there, taught him the prayers and songs he must know, and told him what sacrifices he must make. These must include fragments of turquoise, white shell, haliotis, and cannel-coal, besides destsí corn-pollen and larkspur pollen, and were to be tied up in different bags before he started. "When you get into the plain, as far off as the people of White House can see you, begin to sing one of these songs and a rainbow will form on which you may walk," said *Hastséyalti*.

A TALE OF KININAÉKAI: ACCOUNTING FOR THE ORIGIN
OF CERTAIN PRAYERS AND SONGS OF THE NIGHT CHANT.

http://www.sacred-texts.com/nam/nav/nmps/nmps04.htm

2.3   A Navajo Song

From the base of the east.
From the base of the Pelado Peak.
From the house made of mirage,
From the story made of mirage,
From the doorway of rainbow,
The path out of which is the rainbow,
The rainbow passed out with me.
The rainbow raised up with me.
Through the middle of broad fields,
The rainbow returned with me.
To where my house is visible,
The rainbow returned with me.

To the roof of my house,
The rainbow returned with me.
To the entrance of my house,
The rainbow returned with me.
To just within my house,
The rainbow returned with me.
To my fireside,
The rainbow returned with me.
To the center of my house,
The rainbow returned with me.
At the fore part of my house with the
    dawn,

The Talking God sits with me.
The House God sits with me.
Pollen Boy sits with me.
Grasshopper Girl sits with me.
In beauty Estsánatlehi, my mother, for
    her I return.
Beautifully my fire to me is restored.

Beautifully my possessions are to me
    restored.
Beautifully my soft goods to me are
    restored.
Beautifully my hard goods to me are
    restored.
Beautifully my horses to me are restored.
Beautifully my sheep to me are restored.
Beautifully my old men to me are
    restored.
Beautifully my old women to me are
    restored.
Beautifully my young men to me are
    restored.
Beautifully my women to me are
    restored.
Beautifully my children to me are
    restored.
Beautifully my wife to me is restored.
Beautifully my chiefs to me are restored.
Beautifully my country to me is restored.
Beautifully my fields to me are restored.
Beautifully my house to me is restored.
Talking God sits with me.
House God sits with me.
Pollen Boy sits with me.

Grasshopper Girl sits with me.
Beautifully white corn to me is restored.
Beautifully yellow corn to me is
    restored.
Beautifully blue corn to me is restored.
Beautifully corn of all kinds to me is
    restored.
In beauty may I walk.
All day long may I walk.
Through the returning seasons may I
    walk.
(Translation uncertain.)
Beautifully will I possess again.
(Translation uncertain.)
Beautifully birds . . .
Beautifully joyful birds
On the trail marked with pollen may I
    walk.
With grasshoppers about my feet may I
    walk.
With dew about my feet may I walk.
With beauty may I walk.
With beauty before me, may I walk.
With beauty behind me, may I walk.
With beauty above me, may I walk.
With beauty below me, may, I walk.
With beauty all around me, may I walk.
In old age wandering on a trail of beau-
    ty, lively, may I walk.
In old age wandering on a trail of beau-
    ty, living again, may I walk.
It is finished in beauty.
It is finished in beauty.

A PRAYER OF THE SECOND DAY OF THE NIGHT CHANT

http://www.sacred-texts.com/nam/nav/nmps/nmps05.htm

2.41   A Yoruba Origin Tale

There were no living things
Was the priest of Earth.

That which was suspended,
But did not descend,
Was the priest in heaven.

All was just an empty space
With no substance,
Was the priest of Mid-Air.

It was divined for Earth and Heaven,
When they both existed,
With no inhabitants
In the two empty shells.
There were neither birds nor spirits liv-
      ing in them.

Odumare then created Itself,

Being the Primal cause.
Which is the reason we call Odumare,
The only wise one on earth.
He is the only cause in creation,
The only wise one in heaven, Who creat-
      ed humans.
When He had no companion,
He applied wisdom to the situation
To avert any disaster.

You, alone,
The only one in Heaven
Is the name of Odumare
The only wise open,
We give thanks
The only knowing mind
You created man.
Listening to one side of an argument,
You judged and all are pleased.

Odumare sat back and thought about how to create more things in his universe. For this purpose, he realized he needed more of an intermediary force, since he was to charged with energy to come in direct contact with any living thing and have it survive. Therefore, he created Agbon (wisdom), held it in his palm and thought where it could live. After a while, Odumare released Agbon to fly away and look for a suitable place to lodge. When Agbon could not find a suitable abode, it flew back humming like a bee to Odumare. Odumare took Agbon and swallowed it. Similarly, Imo (knowledge) and Oye (understanding), which were also created, returned for lack of suitable abodes and swallowed for the same reason.

Odumare then "slept," but not in the human sense of the word:

Seemingly asleep but awake,   *their wings against my face.*
Seeming dormant but alive.   *I asked what my offense was,*
Eleye (the witches) swished   *Odumare never slumbers.*

After several thousand years during which Odumare was disturbed by the incessant humming of Agbon, Imo and Oye, he decided to get rid of them in order to have some peace. He order them to descend (ro) making the sound "hoo." Thus the three heavenly bodies now know as Hoo-ro or Oro were evacuated and set for their descent to earth. Since they were heavenly charged life forces from heaven, their descent was accompanied by lighting and thunder. All solid matter melted and became jelly like. For a while, Oro was suspended in mid air like an egg and did not melt, but then it dropped to earth and split (la).

In Oro's new state it is identified with Ela, the deity which functions in the Ifa divination complex and is regarded by the Yoruba as the embodiment of wisdom, knowledge and understanding in all their forms

http://www.anet.net/~ifa/creat_1.htm
http://www.anet.net/~ifa/creat_2.htm

2.42   The Yoruba Circle of Life

The life's circle dramatically shows the cycles one travels between heaven and earth, as we refer to, as Orun and Aiye. This is the existence of all who come into the world and shows the relationship of the Orisa in our journey.

After reincarnating back home, the world is a market place and heaven is home, we reveal our efforts while in the material form. If your character was developed, you elevate into Orisa. If not you prepare to return as Egun. (Do good/speak the truth.)

Next you choose which parents to bring you into the world through the germination of the seed of both parents. Which brings about the order out of what appears to be chaos, the sexual relationship between the "man and woman." That which is the combination of red/blood and white/semen(white blood) in the darkness of the womb, that brings forth light/birth.

Pregnancy state where the child is molded by Kori, the Orisa of children, and Obatala to bring about the harmony out of the darkness and chaos. To establish the moral foundation laid by Olodumare.

After determining the child's makeup/Iwa, Ori is given by Ajalamopin, once chosen by the spirit of the child , then the body and spirit exists in balance. This prepares one for things to come.

You proceed to Aludundun Orun, where one sits with Orunmila and records your destiny. If the new child had once been on earth, rewards for its' good or evil deeds will be incorporated into its' destiny to form part of the Ayanmo.

Before birth, one passes into Odo Aro and Odo Eje. Here all that the person had done in his/her previous life and their choices of destiny is forgotten. This is a warning to do good.

The reminder of the Enikeji, the spiritual double that remains in heaven and reminds one of the convenant made in spirit, some call it deja vu, the separation of spirit and body.

We confront Ogun, who allows us to leave Ikole Orun and into Ikole Aiye. Ogun prepares the road/way from spirit into the material by severing the cord of the womb.

After this stage, we begin our journey in the world. Birth and develop as children, into the adult stage and then back to incarnate home to begin the cycle again unless ones character has elevated. When the fetus is still in the womb, it enjoys both worlds-heaven and earth. The moment one crosses to Odo Aro and Odo Eje, that is its death in Ikole Orun, when the child dies in the womb and when it grows from infancy into old age and passes into the world beyond, that is the death on earth.

This is the path we take and each is responsible for the choices we make. And each will be accountable for all of our deeds. We may believe we can hide from the eyes of Olodumare and justify our selfish motivations, but remember Esu is Olopa Orun and will report all deeds and one will be accountable for those deeds. It's your choice

http://www.anet.net/~ifa/lifecirc.htm

2.43   Yoruba Morning Prayer

I offer you morning greetings in the name of my odu, just as you wake up every morning to offer greetings to Olodumare, the Creator and father of all existence.

I thank you for bringing me to the beginning of another day, for guarding me through my sleep, to see the morning and to look forward to the chores of another day.

I thank you most especially for not allowing me to offend my fellow man, throughout yesterday, because you have ordained, that to serve god, according to the divine laws, your children should be able to tell you, that they have succeeded in resisting temptation, to do any wrongs against olodumare, the two hundred divinities, all the children of God and the society in which they live.

Furthermore, in accordance with your Injunction, I have refrained from avenging all wrongs done to me by my relations, friends and enemies alike.   I thank you for bringing me to the beginning of another day, for guarding me through my sleep, to see the morning and to look forward to the chores of another day.

I thank you most especially for not allowing me to offend my fellow man, throughout yesterday, because you have ordained, that to serve god, according to the divine laws, your children should be able to tell you, that they have succeeded in resisting temptation, to do any wrongs against olodumare, the two hundred divinities, all the children of God and the society in which they live.

Furthermore, in accordance with your Injunction, I have refrained from avenging all wrongs done to me by my relations, friends and enemies alike.

Help me also to neutralize all evil plans against me, just as you will neutralize any evil that I might be tempted to plan against my fellow being. Because as you have proclaimed, that is the universal secret to long life and Enduring prosperity.

Protect me today as always from all dangers And evils in my abode, place of work and in my interactions with others.

http://www.anet.net/~ifa/mornpray.htm

2.5   A Maori Origin Tale

The great mysterious Cause of all things existing in the Cosmos was, as he conceived it, the generative Power. Commencing with a primitive state of Darkness, he conceived Po (=Night) as a person capable of begetting a race of beings resembling itself. After a succession of several generations of the race of Po, Te Ata (=Morn) was given birth to. Then followed certain beings existing when Cosmos was without form, and void. Afterwards came Rangi (=Heaven), Papa (=Earth), the Winds, and other Sky-powers, as are recorded in the genealogical traditions preserved to the present time.

1. That comprising the personified Powers of Nature preceding the existence of man
2. In addition to this the *Maori* had a religious worship peculiar to each tribe and to each family, in forms of *karakia* or invocation addressed to the spirits of dead ancestors of their own proper line of descent.
3. From the time of the migration to New Zealand each tribe and each family would in addition address their invocations to their own proper line of ancestors,—thus giving rise to a family religious worship in addition to the national religion.

The cause of the preservation of their Genealogies becomes intelligible when we consider that they often formed the ground-work of their religious formulas, and that to make an error or even hesitation in repeating a *karakia* was deemed fatal to its efficacy.

In the forms of *karakia* addressed to the spirits of ancestors, the concluding words are generally a petition to the *Atua* invoked to give force or effect to the *karakia* as being derived through the *Tipua*, the *Pukenga*, and the *Whananga*, and so descending to the living *Tauira*.

MAORI COSMOGONY.

Powers of Night and Darkness.	Te Po (= The Night).
	Te Po-teki (= hanging Night).
	Te Po-terea (= drifting Night).
	Te Po-whawha (= moaning Night).
	Hine-ruakimoe
	Te Po.
Powers of Light.	Te Ata (= The Morn).
	Te Ao-tu-roa (= The abiding Day).
	Te Ao-marama (= bright Day).
	Whaitua (=space).

Powers of Cosmos without form and void.	Te Kore (= The Void).
	Te Kore-tuatahi.
	Te Kore-tuarua.
	Kore-nui.
	Kore-roa.
	Kore-para.
	Kore-whiwhia.
	Kore-rawea.
	Kore-te-tamaua (= Void fast bound).
	Te Mangu (= the black) sc. Erebus.

From the union of Te Mangu with Mahorahora nui-a-Rangi (= The great expanse of Rangi) came four children:—

1. Toko-mua (= elder prop).
2. Toko-roto (= middle prop).
3. Toko-pa (= last prop).
4. Rangi-potiki (= child Rangi).

GENEALOGICAL DESCENT FROM TOKO-MUA.

Powers of The Air, Winds.	Tu-awhio-nuku (= Tu of the whirlwind).
	Tu-awhio-rangi.
	Paroro-tea (= white skud).
	Hau-tuia (= piercing wind).
	Hau-ngangana (blustering wind).
	Ngana.
	Ngana-nui.
	Ngana-roa.
	Ngana-ruru.
	Ngana-mawaki.
	Tapa-huru-kiwi.
	Tapa-huru-manu.
	[1] Tiki.
Human beings begin to exist.	Tiki-te-pou-mua (The 1st Man).
	Tiki-te-pou-roto.
	Tiki-haohao.
	Tiki-ahu-papa.
	Te Papa-tutira.
	Ngai.
	Ngai-nui.
	Ngai-roa.

Human beings begin to exist. *(cont'd)*

Ngai-peha.
Te Atitutu.
Te Ati-hapai.
[2] Toi-te-huatahi.
Rauru.
Rutana.

Whatonga.
Apa-apa.
Taha-titi.
Ruatapu.
Rakeora.
Tama-ki-te-ra.
Rongo-maru-a-whatu.
Rere.
Tata =

Wakaotirangi.
Hotumatapu.
Motai.
Ue.
Raka.
Kakati.
Tawhao.
Turongo.
Raukawa.
Wakatere.
Taki-hiku.
Tama-te-hura.
Tui-tao.
Hae.
Nga-tokowaru.

Rongokako.
Tamatea.
[1] Kahu-hunu.

Tamatea was settled at Muriwhenua, and his son Kahuhunu was born there. The latter went on a journey to Nukutauraua near the Mahia, and there married Rongomai-wahine, having got rid of her husband Tamatakutai by craft. Tamatea went to bring him home, but on their return their canoe was upset in a rapid, near where the river Waikato flows out of the lake Taupo, and Tamatea was drowned.

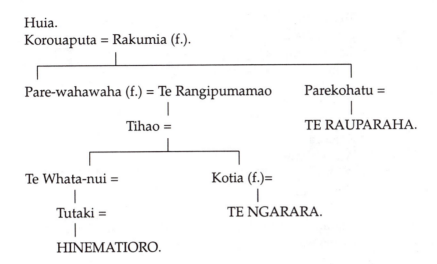

Huia.
Korouaputa = Rakumia (f.).

Pare-wahawaha (f.) = Te Rangipumamao   Parekohatu =

Tihao =   TE RAUPARAHA.

Te Whata-nui =   Kotia (f.)=

Tutaki =   TE NGARARA.

HINEMATIORO.

GENEALOGICAL DESCENT FROM TOKO-ROTO.

Powers of the Heavens.   Rangi-nui.
                                Rangi-roa.
                                Rangi-pouri.
                                Rangi-potango.
                                Rangi-whetu-ma.
                                Rangi-whekere.
                                Ao-nui.
                                Ao-roa.
                                Ao-tara.
                                Urupa.
                                Hoehoe.
                                Puhaorangi (f.).

After the birth of Rauru, the son of Toi-te-huatahi and Kuraemonoa, while Toi was absent from home fishing, Puhaorangi came down from Heaven, andcarried off Kuraemonoa to be his own wife. She bore four children from this union:—

1. Ohomairangi.   2. Tawhirioho.
3. Ohotaretare.   4. Oho-mata-kamokamo.

From Ohomairangi descended:—

Muturangi.
Taunga.

Tuamatua.
Houmaitahiti.
Tama-te-kapua.
Kahu.
Tawaki.
Uenuku.
Rangitihi.
Ratorua.
Wakairikawa.
Waitapu
Hine-rehua.
To Kahu-reremoa.
Waitapu.
Parekawa.
To Kohera.
Pakaki =

Time of
Migration
from
Hawaiki.

To Rangi-pumamao =   Parewahaika = Te Whata

Tihao.   Tokoahu.   Tuiri.
Kotia.   Hihitaua.   Waho (f.).
TE NGARARA.   To Tumuhuia   TE HIRA.
                       or
                    TARAIA.

GENEALOGICAL DESCENT FROM TOKO-PA.

Kohu (=Mist) was the child of Tokopa.
Kohu married To Ika-roa (= The Milky-way), and gave birth to Nga Whetu (= The Stars).

GENEALOGICAL DESCENT FROM RANGI-POTIKI.

Rangi-potiki had three wives, the first of which was Hine-ahu-papa; from her descended:

Sky Powers   Tu-nuku.
                    Tu-rangi.
                    Tama-i-koropao.
                    Haronga.

Haronga took to wife Tongo-tongo. Their children were a son and daughter, Te Ra (= The Sun) and Marama (= The Moon). Haronga perceiving that there was no light for his daughter Marama, gave To Kohu in marriage to Te Ikaroa, and the Stars were born to give light for the sister of To Ra, for the child of Tongo-tongo. "*Nga toko-rua a Tongotongo*" (= the two children of Tongotongo) is a proverbial term for the Sun and Moon at the present day.

Rangi-potiki's third wife was Papa (= Earth). Tangaroa was accused of having committed adultery with Papa, and Rangipotiki, armed with his spear, went to obtain satisfaction. He found Tangaroa seated by the door of his house, who, when he saw Rangi thus coming towards him, began the following *karakia*, at the same time striking his right shoulder with his left hand:—

Tangaroa, Tangaroa,
Tangaroa, unravel;
Unravel the tangle,
Unravel, untwist.

Though Rangi is distant,
He is to be reached.
Some darkness for above,
Some light for below
Freely give
For bright Day

This invocation of Tangaroa was scarce ended when Rangi made a thrust at him. Tangaroa warded it off, and it missed him. Then Tangaroa made a thrust at Rangi, and pierced him quite through the thigh, and he fell.

While Rangi lay wounded he begat his child Kueo (= Moist). The cause of this name was Rangi's wetting his couch while he lay ill of his wound. After Kueo, he begat Mimi-ahi, so-called from his making water by the fireside. Next he begat Tane-tuturi (= straight-leg-Tane), so-called because Rangi could now stretch his legs. Afterwards he begat Tane-pepeki (= bent-leg-Tane), so-called because Rangi could sit with his knees bent. The next child was Tane-ua-tika (= straight-neck Tane), for Rangi's neck was now straight, and he could hold up his head. The next child born was called Tane-ua-ha (= strong-neck-Tane), for Rangi's neck was strong. Then was born Tane-te-waiora, (= lively Tane), so called because Rangi was quite recovered. Then was born Tane-nui-a-Rangi (= Tane great son of Rangi). And last of all was born Paea, a daughter. She was the last of Rangi's children. With Paea they came to an end, so she was named Paea, which signifies 'closed.'

Some time after the birth of these children the thought came to Tane-nui-a-Rangi to separate their father from them. Tane had seen the light of the Sun shining under the armpit of Rangi; so he consulted with his elder brothers what they should do. They all said, "Let us kill our father, because he has shut us up in darkness, and let us leave our mother for our parent." But Tane advised, "Do not let us kill our father, but rather let us raise him up above, so that there may be light." To this they consented; so they prepared ropes, and when Rangi was sound asleep they rolled him over on the ropes, and Paea took him on her back. Two props were also placed under Rangi. The names of the props were Tokohurunuku, and Tokohururangi. Then lifting him with the aid of these two props, they shoved him upwards. Then Papa thus uttered her farewell to Rangi.

"Haera ra, e Rangi, ê! ko le wehenga taua i a Rangi."
"Go, O Rangi, alas! for my separation from Rangi."

And Rangi answered from above:

"Heikona ra, e Papa, ê! ko te wehenga taua i a Papa."
"Remain there, O Papa. Alas! for my separation from Papa."

So Rangi dwelt above, and Tane and his brothers dwelt below with their mother, Papa.

Some time after this Tane desired to have his mother Papa for his wife. But Papa said, "Do not turn your inclination towards me, for evil will come to you. Go to your ancestor Mumuhango." So Tane took Mumuhango to wife, who brought forth the *totara* tree. Tane returned to his mother dissatisfied, and his mother said, "Go to your ancestor Hine-tu-a-maunga (= the mountain maid)." So Tane took Hine-tu-a-maunga to wife, who conceived, but did not bring forth a child. Her offspring was the rusty water of mountains, and the monster reptiles common to mountains. Tane was displeased, and returned to his mother. Papa said to him "Go to your ancestor Rangahore." So Tane went, and took that female for a wife, who brought forth stone. This greatly displeased Tane, who again went back to Papa. Then Papa said "Go to your ancestor Ngaore (= the tender one). Tane took Ngaore to wife. And Ngaore gave birth to the *toetoe* (a species of rush-like grass). Tane returned to his mother in displeasure. She next advised him, "Go to your ancestor Pakoti." Tane did as he was bid, but Pakoti only brought forth *hareheke* (= phormium tenax). Tane had a great many other wives at his mother's bidding, but none of them pleased him, and his heart was greatly troubled, because no child was born to give birth to Man; so he thus addressed his mother—"Old lady, there will never be any progeny for me." Thereupon Papa said, "Go to your ancestor, Ocean, who is grumbling there in the distance. When you reach the beach at Kura-waka, gather up the earth in the form of man." So Tane went and scraped up the earth at Kura-waka. He gathered up the earth, the body was formed, and then the head, and the arms; then he joined on the legs, and patted down the surface of the belly, so as to give the form of man; and when he had done this, he returned to his mother and said, "The whole body of the man is finished." Thereupon his mother said, "Go to your ancestor Mauhi, she will give the *raho*. Go to your ancestor Whete, she will give the *timutimu*. Go to your ancestor Taua-ki-te-marangai, she will give the *paraheka*. Go to your ancestor Punga-heko, she has the *huruhuru*." So Tane went to these female ancestors, who gave him the things asked for. He then went to Kura-waka. Katahi ka whakanoho ia i nga raho ki roto i nga kuwha o te wahine i hanga ki to one: Ka man era. Muri atu ka whakanoho ia ko to timutimu na Whete i homai ki waenga i nga raho; muri atu ko to paraheka na Taua-ki-te-marangai i homai ka whakanoho ki to take o to timutimu: muri iho ko to huruhuru na Pungaheko i homai ka whakanoho ki runga i to puke. Ka oti, katahi ka tapa ko Hineahuone. Then he named this female form Hine-ahu-one (= The earth formed maid).

Tane took Hine-ahu-one to wife. She first gave birth to Tiki-tohua—the egg of a bird from which have sprung all the birds of the air. After that, Tikikapakapa was born-a female. Then first was born for Tane a human child. Tane took great care of Tikikapakapa, and when she grew up he gave her a new name, Hine-a-tauira (= the pattern maid). Then he took her to wife, and she bore a female child who was named Hine-titamauri.

One day Hine-a-tauira said to Tane, "Who is my father?" Tane laughed. A second time Hine-a-tauira asked the same question. Then Tane made a sign:

and the woman understood, and her heart was dark, and she gave herself up to mourning, and fled away to Rikiriki, and to Naonao, to Rekoreko, to Waewae-te-Po, and to Po.[1] The woman fled away, hanging down her head. [2]Then she took the name of Hine-nui-te-Po (= great woman of Night). Her farewell words to Tane were—"Remain, O Tane, to pull up our offspring to Day; while I go below to drag down our offspring to Night."[3]

Tane sorrowed for his daughter-wife, and cherished his daughter Hinetitamauri; and when she grew up he gave her to Tiki to be his wife, and their first-born child was Tiki-te-pou-mua.

The following narrative is a continuation of the history of Hinenuitepo from another source:—

After Hinenuitepo fled away to her ancestors in the realms of Night, she gave birth to Te Po-uriuri (= The Dark one), and to Te Po-tangotango (= The very dark), and afterwards to Pare-koritawa, who married Tawaki, one of the race of Rangi. Hence the proverb when the sky is seen covered with small clouds *"Parekoritawa is tilling her garden."* When Tawaki climbed to Heaven with Pareko-ritawa, he repeated this *karakia.*:—

Ascend, O Tawaki, by the narrow path,
By which the path of Rangi was followed;
The path of Tu-kai-te-uru.

When Tawaki and Parekoritawa mounted to the Sky, they left behind them a token—a black moth—a token of the mortal body.

Pare gave birth to Uenuku (= Rainbow). Afterwards she brought forth Whatitiri (= Thunder). Hence the rainbow in the sky, and the thunder-clap.

Notes

1. These were all ancestors of the race of Powers of Night.
2. *He oti, ka rere te wahine: ka anga ko te pane ki raro, tuwhera tonu nga kuwha, hamama tonu te pua-
pua.*
3. *"Heikona, e Tane, hei kukume ake i a taua hua ki te Ao; kia haere au ki raro hei kukume iho i a taua
hua ki te Po."*
4. Vid. Genealogical Table.]
    The narrow path is climbed,
    The broad path is climbed,
    The path by which was followed
    Your ancestors, Te Aonui,
    Te Ao-roa,
    Te Ao-whititera.
    Now you mount up
    To your *Ihi,*
    To your *Mana,*
    To the Thousands above,
    To your *Ariki,*
    To your *Tapairu,*
    To your *Pukenga,*
    To your *Whananga,*
    To your *Tauira.*

MAORI COSMOGONY AND MYTHOLOGY.

http://www.sacred-texts.com/pac/mrm/mrm04.htm

2.6 Indigenous Sacred Ways in the Modern World

A Conversation Between Native American and Maori Spiritual Leaders

Macki Ruka is an international speaker and healer, chosen at age three to be initiated into the highest teachings of the celestial and earthly realms. He was chosen by the United Nations as one of seven elders to take ancient prophecies to the world. Macki has traveled around the world five times in his journey, meeting with the Pope, the Dali Lama, Mother Theresa, and other world spiritual leaders. He has led journeys and ceremonies at sacred sites around the world such as Machu Picchu, Israel, India, China, Russia, and Egypt. The Waitaha Maoris are a matriarchal culture. Macki is a grandson in the line of the current Matriarch. He has lived all his life in "priestly" functions, performing ancient ceremonial rituals that have been part of his culture for over 500,000 years.

Cherokee Jim Elder Yellow Horse Man joins Mac in his quest for the prophecies. He has been traveling with Macki through the country and New Zealand doing a lot of work, bringing out a message. He is a medicine man.

In June of 1996 I attended the first Star Knowledge Conference in Marty, South Dakota. Macki Ruka was a presenter who enlightened many people with his words and energies.

EC: Yellow Horse Man ("YH"), what were your experiences in New Zealand?

YH: I got to meet Macki's people, the Waitaha, meaning the water carriers. There I saw a beautiful dance that was being created from the grandmothers and the sisters. The dance has gone on for hundreds of thousands of years. I was taken to their beautiful ceremonial houses. The walls were carved with the genology that dates back 500,000 years ago. Up on the ceiling were the star charts.It takes them all the way back to the planet that they came here from. From working with these people, I came to understand brother Macki's message that he is carrying throughout the world. I learned that brother Macki is completing the prophies of 500,000 years. He has been to all the sacred sites around the world.

EC: Where was his most current journey?

YH: His most current journey was Egypt. There he completed a ceremony that his people had been holding off for a certain period of time. There had to be a correct time for the ceremony to be completed. This time was shown to them.He was the one of the Waitaha people chosen to go out into the world to perform these sacred ceremonies. The name of this ceremony is "unveiling of the Goddess". This is the opening up of the Matriarchal society throughout the world. That particular ceremony had brought Macki to the United States.

EC: Where did Macki get his training?

YH: He was trained by the Matriachs of his tribe, the grandmothers. They taught him all of the genelogy, knowledge, and wisdom — the ceremonies, the stories, the songs, and the incantations. At age seven, he swam with dolphins and whales. These ceremonies have been handed down through oral tradition with the indigeous peoples of his tribe. Grandmother, woman is the carrier of the seed of knowledge. The ceremony enhances the power of women, the life givers. Men and women should be in balance.

EC: How did you know that you would meet Macki Ruka?

YH: A grandmother from the Cree Nation, up in Canada, had a dream. When she meet Macki, she told him that she had this dream and that there was a man that he would meet. That was the first time Macki ever worked with anyone. He listened to the grandmother's dream. This grandmother came up and saw me since I had known her before. This was at the sundance in South Dakota. When I met

Macki, it was like we had known each other for thousands of years. Our prophecies coincide with each other. This is the great time of preparation. We started working together last year in Seattle, Washington. Since then we have worked with thousands of people in thousands of ceremonies all over the United States. I would like to introduce you to Macki Ruka.

EC: Hello Macki Ruka ("MR").

MR: I am honored that we have this opportunity to speak, to be here on this planet now, mother earth, to share the beauty of her abundance, and to see that amazing white light that is the giver and enhancer of all that is within the peace of man.

EC: Could you tell us more about your work?

MR: I am a TUMULA??, like a medicine man but with a wider scope, the speaker of the dead, the teller of the stories, the keeper of ancient wisdom, who operates the vibrations of healing, transmuting the energies. I am a doctor, a midwife, I am everything that is the essence of survival of my tribe or you may call it a community. My education became mother earth. My mentor was the Matriarch of our culture, my grandmother. She was the keeper of the ancient wisdom. Women are the builders of men. Sisters are the spring of emotion. Mother earth, mother nature holds the frequency of the ecosystem. Mother moon is grandmother.

EC: What changes are occuring on the planet now?

MR: The trees are dying from the tops down. Frogs are being born with deformities. We see the animal kingdom all changing. This is not just in one country but through out the world. We see coming towards us all these strange diseases and sicknesses. We see the Bubonic and the Pneumonic Plagues in India. We see how the very air we breathe is destroying us. All this is part of the great prophecy of all time. We see the coming of new energies in the solar system. We see what they bring for us. We believe whatever the situation that you are in that you vibrate to creates cause and effect ... Karma. You'll get back whatever you give out. If you give out love, it will come back ten fold. This applies for other emotions. Now is the time to find the beauty of out hearts, that soul seat. Tome to start repairing it ... . that torn thread of the soul. The spirit has been tattered and now it is up to us to find that. Find the golden thread and needle and use it to heal the torn thread of the garment. The thread comes from the sacred garment of Creator. Repair the soul with the love of the creator. Then you dance with the beauty of "self", you become the enhancer. You have the memory of knowing your past lives of ancient times.

EC: Is this becoming One with the Universe?

MR: Exactly! First we must become One with ourselves. We say that the longest journey is from the mind to the heart. Longer still, is that very journey that takes us back from the heart to the mind. Here begins the sacred of all journeys ... . all experiences in one's life. This is a teaching.

EC: What are the future prophecies?

MR: Doom and gloom! We see great changes in the weather. We see water upon water upon water. The changing of the climate of the great mother earth, and the shifting. The coming of the Millenium, the year 2000, we see the changes in the structures of government. The fall of the monetary system. We see a time of beauty. We are living in the time of chaos, technology, where technology has left man behind. This is the sad part. Technology is leaving us so far behind. Billions and Billions of dollars to create one plane. This money could feed thousands of childrens in many, many countries.

EC: Can this be prevented?

MR: This is a good story. First we must find the beauty of self within our hearts. Once there find the compassion. Compassion is an act of power. We are not here to heal the good and the bad, we are not here to make the wrong right, we are here for one purpose ... .. to find the constancy of the truth. The universal truth is with great spirit, creator. That is our devine right to enhance the heart and find the beauty, thereby radiating that beauty to other people. Giving back to the people is where we begin the first prophecy that heals the rest.

EC: Can you tell us about the prophecies?

MR: The first prophecy is the unity with self and the universe. The second is to begin as the seperation of the witnesses. You be the witnesses. You stand there and witness the great unification that you are doing with people, with your friends and family, with other people that you come in contact with. With the God child within each one of us. Three, honoring that God child within yourself thereby honoring other people that come in contact with you. Four is to see through meditation, the artistic works of great spirit. That is the ecosystem or mother nature. Use mother nature to heal the hurts within ourselves. There the witnessing begins of the unification. Five is the free gift of grace given to man. Grace is that feminity within the feminine. Grace is the Goddess, Shekinah, Sophia the Goddess of compassion. Six the most beautiful gift of all is unconditional love. Honor one another in the way we love. Learn when to let go. Learn not to possess or control. Seven is the Holy Trinity ... the great number of creator ... the beauty that is enhancing the devine in all ... brings in the joy and the love and the light of great spirit. Eight is the forever energy of the Christ Consciousness ... the vibration and love that we have for one another ... Uncondtional love. Nine is now, now and forever more. Ten is the perfection of great spirit. Eleven is the chaos we are going through and yet we will find the balance. Twelve is the order of perfection of what is to come. to this beautiful mother earth to make heaven on earth.

EC: Are your ceremonies with men and women?

MR: I work with men and women all over the world.

EC: What do you do at a ceremony?

MR: I begin with the initiation of the heart. I try to stop the "mind chatter". This is different than meditation which last for a short time then you process and go back to your normal life. I give them the gift of finding things that people take with them every second, every minute, every hour, every day of their lives. They carry the love and become the teacher. They teach themselves and bring it to others.

EC: Is this a simple thing to do?

MR: Yes. It is simple. Everything done in creation is done with simplicity. It is man and his complicated mind that have made things very difficult. We are eating from the "Tree of Illusion".

EC: What happens during a ceremony?

MR: People sit in a sacred circle of 12. I use the sacred colors of the rainbow to the 12 celestial realms. Some of the ceremonies are: Full Moon, New Moon, Opening the Chakras, Opening the Heart, to mother earth among others. Spirit guides the right people to the ceremonies.

EC: What tools do you use?

MR: I carry my altar everywhere I go. Part of my job is to reactiviate the energies in the ancient temples. I travel with a lot of special sisters (women) from around the world. I call them angels. Spirit send them to me for this reactivation in the ancient temples that were built to honor the Goddess. From Peru, to the Yucatan, to Bolivia, to Macchu Picchu, the Anastazi, the Hopi, the Cherokee, the Lakota, all around the world. Some of the great chief and grandmothers chose to leave now to work on the other side. I see the beauty of the wisdom of the grandmother and I honor that throughout the world.

EC: What is your forte?

MR: The celestial bodies ... the stars.

EC: In conclusion what is your final message to the readers?

MR: I have been brought up in the matriarch system That is where the wisdom is. May you be as gentle as the flight of the butterfly. All those that read this message ... let them have the eyes to see and the ears to hear. Listen to the message and not the messenger.

EC: Thank you.

MR: Thank you, Ellie. It is a joy to share energies with you.

http://www.crystalinks.com/macki.html

Hinduism

3.1 Selections from the Rig Veda

3.11 Invocation of Angi

1 I Laud Agni, the chosen Priest, God, minister of sacrifice,
The hotar, lavishest of wealth.

2 Worthy is Agni to be praised by living as by ancient seers.
He shall bring. hitherward the Gods.

3 Through Agni man obtaineth wealth, yea, plenty waxing day by day,
Most rich in heroes, glorious.

4 Agni, the perfect sacrifice which thou encompassest about
Verily goeth to the Gods.

5 May Agni, sapient-minded Priest, truthful, most gloriously great,
The God, come hither with the Gods.

6 Whatever blessing, Agni, thou wilt grant unto thy worshipper,
That, Angiras, is indeed thy truth.

7 To thee, dispeller of the night, O Agni, day by day with prayer
Bringing thee reverence, we come

8 Ruler of sacrifices, guard of Law eternal, radiant One,
Increasing in thine own abode.

9 Be to us easy of approach, even as a father to his son:
Agni, be with us for our weal.

http://www.hinduwebsite.com/sacredscripts/rig_veda_book_1.htm
The RIG VEDA
Ralph T.H. Griffith, translator 1889

3.12   The Sacrifice of Purusha

1 A THOUSAND heads hath Purusa, a thousand eyes, a thousand feet.
On every side pervading earth he fills a space ten fingers wide.

2 This Purusa is all that yet hath been and all that is to be;
The Lord of Immortality which waxes greater still by food.

3 So mighty is his greatness; yea, greater than this is Purusa.
All creatures are one-fourth of him, three-fourths eternal life in heaven.

4 With three-fourths Purusa went up: onefourth of him again was here.
Thence he strode out to every side over what cats not and what cats.

5 From him Viraj was born; again Purusa from Viraj was born.
As soon as he was born he spread eastward and westward o'er the earth.

6 When Gods prepared the sacrifice with Purusa as their offering,
Its oil was spring, the holy gift was autumn; summer was the wood.

7 They balmed as victim on the grass Purusa born in earliest time.
With him the Deities and all Sadhyas and Rsis sacrificed.

8 From that great general sacrifice the dripping fat was gathered up.
He formed the creatures of-the air, and animals both wild and tame.

9 From that great general sacrifice Rcas and Sama-hymns were born:
Therefrom were spells and charms produced; the Yajus had its birth from it.

10 From it were horses born, from it all cattle with two rows of teeth:
From it were generated kine, from it the goats and sheep were born.

11 When they divided Purusa how many portions did they make?
What do they call his mouth, his arms? What do they call his thighs and feet?

12 The Brahman was his mouth, of both his arms was the Rajanya made.
His thighs became the Vaisya, from his feet the Sudra was produced.

13 The Moon was gendered from his mind, and from his eye the Sun had birth;
Indra and Agni from his mouth were born, and Vayu from his breath.

14 Forth from his navel came mid-air the sky was fashioned from his head
Earth from his feet, and from his car the regions. Thus they formed the worlds.

15 Seven fencing-sticks had he, thrice seven layers of fuel were prepared,
When the Gods, offering sacrifice, bound, as their victim, Purusa.

16 Gods, sacrificing, sacrificed the victim these were the earliest holy ordinances.

The Mighty Ones attained the height of heaven, there where the Sidhyas, Gods of old,
are dwelling.

http://www.sacred-texts.com/hin/rigveda/rv10090.htm
The RIG VEDA,
Ralph T.H. Griffith, translator 1889

3.13 An Origin Tale from the Rig Veda

1 THEN was not non-existent nor existent: there was no realm of air, no sky beyond it.
What covered in, and where? and what gave shelter? Was water there, unfathomed
depth of water?

2 Death was not then, nor was there aught immortal: no sign was there, the day's and
night's divider.
That One Thing, breathless, breathed by its own nature: apart from it was nothing
whatsoever.

3 Darkness there was: at first concealed in darknew this All was indiscriminated
chaos.
All that existed then was void and form less: by the great power of Warmth was
born that Unit.

4 Thereafter rose Desire in the beginning, Desire, the primal seed and germ of Spirit. Sages who searched with their heart's thought discovered the existent's kinship in the non-existent.

5 Transversely was their severing line extended: what was above it then, and what below it?
There were begetters, there were mighty forces, free action here and energy up yonder

6 Who verily knows and who can here declare it, whence it was born and whence comes this creation?
TheGods are later than this world's production. Who knows then whence it first came into being?

7 He, the first origin of this creation, whether he formed it all or did not form it, Whose eye controls this world in highest heaven, he verily knows it, or perhaps he knows not.

http://www.sacred-texts.com/hin/rigveda/rv10129.htm
The RIG VEDA, Ralph T.H. Griffith, translator 1889

3.2 Selections from the Upanishads

BRIHADARANYAKA-UPANISHAD Part 1

FIRST ADHYAYA: FIRST BRAHMANA.

Verily the dawn is the head of the horse which is fit for sacrifice, the sun its eye, the wind its breath, the mouth the Vaisvanara fire, the year the body of the sacrificial horse. Heaven is the back, the sky the belly, the earth the chest, the quarters the two sides, the intermediate quarters the ribs, the members the seasons, the joints the months and half-months, the feet days and nights, the bones the stars, the flesh the clouds. The half-digested food is the sand, the rivers the bowels, the liver and the lungs the mountains, the hairs the herbs and trees. As the sun rises, it is the forepart, as it sets, the hindpart of the horse. When the horse shakes itself, then it lightens; when it kicks, it thunders; when it makes water, it rains; voice is its voice.

Verily Day arose after the horse as the (golden) vessel, called Mahiman (great-ness), which (at the sacrifice) is placed before the horse. Its place is in the Eastern sea. The Night arose after the horse, as the (silver) vessel, called Mahiman, which (at the sacrifice) is placed behind the horse. Its place is in the Western sea. Verily, these two vessels (or greatnesses) arose to be on each side of the horse.

As a racer he carried the Devas, as a stallion the Gandharvas, as a runner the Asuras, as a horse men. The sea is its kin, the sea is its birthplace.

In the beginning there was nothing (to be perceived) here whatsoever. By Death indeed all this was concealed,-by hunger; for death is hunger. Death (the first being) thought, 'Let me have a body.' Then he moved about, worshipping. From him thus worshipping water was produced. And he said: 'Verily, there appeared to me, while I worshipped (arkate), water (ka).' This is why water is called ar-ka. Surely there is water (or pleasure) for him who thus knows the reason why water is called arka.

There were two kinds of descendants of Pragapati, the Devas and the Asuras. Now the Devas were indeed the younger, the Asuras the elder ones. The Devas, who were struggling in these worlds, said: 'Well, let us overcome the Asuras at the sacri-fices (the Gyotishtoma) by means of the udgitha.'

They said to speech (Vak): 'Do thou sing out for us (the udgitha).' 'Yes,' said speech, and sang (the udgitha). Whatever delight there is in speech, that she obtained for the Devas by singing (the three pavamanas); but that she pronounced well (in the other nine pavamanas), that was for herself. The Asuras knew: 'Verily, through this singer they will overcome us.' They therefore rushed at the singer and pierced her with evil. That evil which consists in saying what is bad, that is that evil.

Then they (the Devas) said to breath (scent): 'Do thou sing out for us.' 'Yes,' said breath, and sang. Whatever delight there is in breath (smell), that he obtained for the Devas by singing; but that he smelled well, that was for himself. The Asuras knew: 'Verily, through this singer they will overcome us.' They therefore rushed at the singer, and pierced him with evil. That evil which consists in smelling what is bad, that is that evil.

Then they said to the eye: 'Do thou sing out for us.' 'Yes,' said the eye, and sang. Whatever delight there is in the eye, that he obtained for the Devas by singing; but that he saw well, that was for himself. The Asuras knew: 'Verily, through this singer they will overcome us.'

Max Müllers' translation of the Upanishads, Volume Two. (1884)
(Volume 15 of the Sacred Books of the East.)
http://www.hinduwebsite.com/sacredscripts/brihad_max1.htm

3.3 The Laws of Manu and the Stages of Life

The vow (of studying) the three Vedas under a teacher must be kept for thirty-six years, or for half that time, or for a quarter, or until the (student) has perfectly learnt them.

(A student) who has studied in due order the three Vedas, or two, or even one only, without breaking the (rules of) studentship, shall enter the order of householders.

He who is famous for (the strict performance of) his duties and has received his heritage, the Veda, from his father, shall be honoured, sitting on a couch and adorned with a garland, with (the present of) a cow (and the honey-mixture).

Having bathed, with the permission of his teacher, and performed according to the rule the Samavartana (the rite on returning home), a twice-born man shall marry a wife of equal caste who is endowed with auspicious (bodily) marks.

A damsel who is neither a Sapinda on the mother's side, nor belongs to the same family on the father's side, is recommended to twice-born men for wedlock and conjugal union.

In connecting himself with a wife, let him carefully avoid the ten following families, be they ever so great, or rich in kine, horses, sheep, grain, or (other) property,

(Viz.) one which neglects the sacred rites, one in which no male children (are born), one in which the Veda is not studied, one (the members of) which have thick hair on the body, those which are subject to hemorrhoids, phthisis, weakness of digestion, epilepsy, or white or black leprosy.

Having dwelt with a teacher during the fourth part of (a man's) life, a Brahmana shall live during the second quarter (of his existence) in his house, after he has wedded a wife.

A Brahmana must seek a means of subsistence which either causes no, or at least little pain (to others), and live (by that) except in times of distress.

For the purpose of gaining bare subsistence, let him accumulate property by (following those) irreproachable occupations (which are prescribed for) his (caste), without (unduly) fatiguing his body.

He may subsist by Rita (truth), and Amrita (ambrosia), or by Mrita (death) and by Pramrita (what causes many deaths); or even by (the mode) called Satyanrita (a mixture of truth and falsehood), but never by Svavritti (a dog's mode of life).

By Rita shall be understood the gleaning of corn; by Amrita, what is given unasked; by Mrita, food obtained by begging and agriculture is declared to be Pramrita.

But trade and (money-lending) are Satyanrita, even by that one may subsist. Service is called Svavritti; therefore one should avoid it.

He may either possess enough to fill a granary, or a store filling a grain-jar; or he may collect what suffices for three days, or make no provision for the morrow.

Moreover, among these four Brahmana householders, each later-(named) must be considered more distinguished, and through his virtue to have conquered the world more completely.

One of these follows six occupations, another subsists by three, one by two, but the fourth lives by the Brahmasattra.

He who maintains himself by picking up grains and ears of corn, must be always intent on (the performance of) the Agnihotra, and constantly offer those Ishtis only, which are prescribed for the days of the conjunction and opposition (of the moon), and for the solstices.

Let him never, for the sake of subsistence, follow the ways of the world; let him live the pure, straightforward, honest life of a Brahmana.

He who desires happiness must strive after a perfectly contented disposition and control himself; for happiness has contentment for its root, the root of unhappiness is the contrary (disposition).

A Brahmana, who is a Snataka and subsists by one of the (above-mentioned) modes of life, must discharge the (following) duties which secure heavenly bliss, long life, and fame.

Let him, untired, perform daily the rites prescribed for him in the Veda; for he who performs those according to his ability, attains to the highest state.

Whether he be rich or even in distress, let him not seek wealth through pursuits to which men cleave, nor by forbidden occupations, nor (let him accept presents) from any (giver whosoever he may be).

Let him not, out of desire (for enjoyments), attach himself to any sensual pleasures, and let him carefully obviate an excessive attachment to them, by (reflecting on their worthlessness in) his heart.

A twice-born Snataka, who has thus lived according to the law in the order of householders, may, taking a firm resolution and keeping his organs in subjection, dwell in the forest, duly (observing the rules given below).

When a householder sees his (skin) wrinkled, and (his hair) white, and. the sons of his sons, then he may resort to the forest.

Abandoning all food raised by cultivation, and all his belongings, he may depart into the forest, either committing his wife to his sons, or accompanied by her.

Taking with him the sacred fire and the implements required for domestic (sacrifices), he may go forth from the village into the forest and reside there, duly controlling his senses.

Let him offer those five great sacrifices according to the rule, with various kinds of pure food fit for ascetics, or with herbs, roots, and fruit.

Let him wear a skin or a tattered garment; let him bathe in the evening or in the morning; and let him always wear (his hair in) braids, the hair on his body, his beard, and his nails (being unclipped).

Let him perform the Bali-offering with such food as he eats, and give alms according to his ability; let him honour those who come to his hermitage with alms consisting of water, roots, and fruit.

Let him be always industrious in privately reciting the Veda; let him be patient of hardships, friendly (towards all), of collected mind, ever liberal and never a receiver of gifts, and compassionate towards all living creatures.

The Laws of Manu, George Bühler, translator
(Sacred Books of the East, Volume 25)
http://www.sacred-texts.com/hin/manu.htm

3.4   Selections from The Bhagavad-Gita

18. Liberation Through Renunciation

Arjun said: I wish to know the nature of Samnyaas and Tyaag and the difference between the two, O Lord Krishn. (18.01)

Definition of renunciation and sacrifice

The Supreme Lord said: The sages call Samnyaas (Renunciation) the complete renunciation of work for personal profit. The wise define Tyaag (Sacrifice) as the sacrifice of, and the freedom from, a selfish attachment to the fruits of all work. (See also 5.01, 5.05, and 6.01) (18.02) Some philosophers say that all work is full of faults and should be given up, while others say that acts of sacrifice, charity, and austerity should not be abandoned. (18.03)

O Arjun, listen to My conclusion about sacrifice. Sacrifice is said to be of three types. (18.04) Acts of service, charity, and austerity should not be abandoned, but should be performed because service, charity, and austerity are the purifiers of the wise. (18.05) Even these obligatory works should be performed without attachment to the fruits. This is My definite supreme advice, O Arjun. (18.06)

Three types of sacrifice

Giving up one's duty is not proper. The abandonment of obligatory work is due to delusion and is declared to be in the mode of ignorance. (18.07) One who abandons duty merely because it is difficult or because of fear of bodily affliction, does not get the benefits of sacrifice by performing such a sacrifice in the mode of passion. (18.08) Obligatory work performed as duty, renouncing selfish attachment to the fruit, is alone to be regarded as sacrifice in the mode of goodness, O Arjun. (18.09) One who neither hates a disagreeable work, nor is attached to an agreeable work, is considered a renunciant (Tyaagi), imbued with the mode of goodness, intelligent, and free from all doubts about the Supreme Being. (18.10) Human beings cannot completely abstain from work. Therefore, one who completely renounces selfish attachment to the fruits of all work is considered a renunciant. (18.11) The threefold fruit of works—desirable, undesirable, and mixed—accrues after death to the one who is not a Tyaagi (Renunciant), but never to a Tyaagi. (18.12)

Five causes of an action

Learn from Me, O Arjun, the five causes, as described in the Saamkhya doctrine, for the accomplishment of all actions. They are: The physical body, the seat of Karm; the modes (Gunas) of material Nature, the doer; the eleven organs of perception and action, the instruments; various Praanas (bioimpulses, life forces); and the fifth is presiding deities (of the eleven organs). (18.13-14) These are the five causes of whatever action, whether right or wrong, one performs by thought, word and deed. (18.15) Therefore, the ignorant, who consider one's body or the soul as the sole agent, do not understand due to imperfect knowledge. (18.16) One who is free from the notion of doership and whose intellect is not polluted by the desire to reap the fruit—even after slaying all these people—neither slays nor is bound by the act of killing. (18.17) The subject, the object, and the knowledge of the object are the threefold driving force (or impetus) to an action. The eleven organs (of perception and action), the act, and the agent or the modes (Gunas) of material Nature are the three components of action. (18.18)

Three types of knowledge

Jnaan (Self-knowledge), Karm (Action), and Kartaa (Agent) are said to be of three types, according to the Guna theory of Saamkhya doctrine. Hear duly about these also. (18.19) The knowledge by which one sees a single immutable Reality in all beings as undivided in the divided, such knowledge is in the mode of goodness. (See also 11.13, and 13.16) (18.20) The knowledge by which one sees different realities of various types among all beings as separate from one another; such knowledge is in the mode of passion. (18.21) The irrational, baseless, and worthless knowledge by which one clings to one single effect (such as the body) as if it is everything, such knowledge is declared to be in the mode of darkness of ignorance. (18.22)

Three types of action

Obligatory duty performed without likes and dislikes and without selfish motives and attachment to enjoy the fruit, is said to be in the mode of goodness. (18.23) Action performed with ego, with selfish motives, and with too much effort, is in the mode of passion. (18.24) Action that is undertaken because of delusion, disregarding consequences, loss, injury to others, as well as one's own ability, is said to be in the mode of ignorance. (18.25)

Three types of agent

The agent who is free from attachment, is non-egotistic, endowed with resolve and enthusiasm, and unperturbed in success or failure is called good. (18.26) The agent who is impassioned, who desires the fruits of work, who is greedy, violent, impure, and gets affected by joy and sorrow; is called passionate. (18.27) The agent who is undisciplined, vulgar, stubborn, wicked, malicious, lazy, depressed, and procrastinating is called ignorant. (18.28)

Three types of intellect

Now hear Me explain fully and separately, O Arjun, the threefold division of intellect and resolve, based on modes of material Nature. (18.29) O Arjun, that intellect is in the mode of goodness which understands the path of work and the path of renunciation, right and wrong action, fear and fearlessness, bondage and liberation. (18.30) That intellect is in the mode of passion which cannot distinguish between righteousness (Dharm) and unrighteousness (Adharm), and right and wrong action, O Arjun. (18.31) That intellect is in the mode of ignorance which, when covered by ignorance, accepts unrighteousness (Adharm) as righteousness (Dharm) and thinks everything to be that which it is not, O Arjun. (18.32)

Three types of resolve, and the four goals of human life

That resolve is in the mode of goodness by which one manipulates the functions of the mind, Praan (bioimpulses, life forces) and senses for God-realization only, O Arjun. (18.33) That resolve is in the mode of passion by which one, craving for the fruits of work, clings to Dharm (Duty), Arth (Wealth), and Kaam (Pleasure) with great attachment. (18.34) That resolve is in the mode of ignorance by which a dull person does not give up sleep, fear, grief, despair, and carelessness, O Arjun. (18.35)

Three types of pleasure

And now hear from Me, O Arjun, about the threefold pleasure. The pleasure that one enjoys from spiritual practice results in cessation of all sorrows. (18.36) The pleasure that appears as poison in the beginning, but is like nectar in the end, comes by the grace of Self-knowledge and is in the mode of goodness. (18.37) Sensual pleasures that appear as nectars in the beginning, but become poison in the end, are in the mode of passion. (See also 5.22) (18.38) Pleasure that confuses a person in the beginning and in the end as a result of sleep, laziness, and carelessness, is in the mode of ignorance. (18.39) There is no being, either on the earth or among the celestial controllers (Devas) in the heaven, who can remain free from these three modes (Gunas) of material Nature (Prakriti). (18.40)

Division of labor is based on one's ability

The division of labor into the four categories—Braahman, Kshatriya, Vaishya, and Shudr—is also based on the qualities inherent in people's nature (or the natural propensities, and not necessarily as one's birth right), O Arjun. (See also 4.13) (18.41) Intellectuals who have serenity, self-control, austerity, purity, patience, honesty, transcendental knowledge, transcendental experience, and belief in God are labeled as Braahmans. (18.42) Those having the qualities of heroism, vigor, firmness, dexterity, steadfastness in battle, charity, and administrative skills are called Kshatriyas or protectors. (18.43) Those who are good at cultivation, cattle rearing, business, trade, and industry are known as Vaishyas. Those who are very good in service and labor type work are classed as Shudras. (18.44)

Attainment of salvation through duty, discipline, and devotion

One can attain the highest perfection by devotion to one's natural work. Listen to Me how one attains perfection while engaged in one's natural work. (18.45) One attains perfection by worshipping the Supreme Being—from whom all beings originate, and by whom all this universe is pervaded—through performance of one's natural duty for Him. (See also 9.27, 12.10) (18.46) One's inferior natural work is better than superior unnatural work even though well performed. One who does the work ordained by one's inherent nature (without selfish motives) incurs no sin (or Karmic reaction). (See also 3.35) (18.47) One's natural work, even though defective, should not be abandoned, because all undertakings are enveloped by defects as fire is covered by smoke, O Arjun. (18.48) The person whose mind is always free from selfish attachment, who has subdued the mind and senses, and who is free from desires, attains the supreme perfection of freedom from the bondage of Karm by renouncing selfish attachment to the fruits of work. (18.49)

Learn from Me briefly, O Arjun, how one who has attained such perfection (or the freedom from the bondage of Karm) attains the Supreme Person, the goal of transcendental knowledge. (18.50) Endowed with purified intellect, subduing the mind with firm resolve, turning away from sound and other objects of the senses, giving up likes and dislikes; living in solitude; eating lightly; controlling the mind, speech, and organs of action; ever absorbed in yog of meditation; taking refuge in detachment;

and relinquishing egotism, violence, pride, lust, anger, and proprietorship—one becomes peaceful, free from the notion of "I" and "my," and fit for attaining oneness with the Supreme Being (ParBrahm). (18.51-53) Absorbed in the Supreme Being (ParBrahm), the serene one neither grieves nor desires. Becoming impartial to all beings, one obtains My Paraa-Bhakti, the highest devotional love. (18.54) By devotion one truly understands what and who I am in essence. Having known Me in essence, one immediately merges with Me. (See also 5.19) (18.55)

A KarmaYogi devotee attains Moksh, the eternal immutable abode, by My grace—even while doing all duties—just by taking refuge in Me (by surrendering all action to Me with loving devotion). (18.56) Sincerely offer all actions to Me, set Me as your supreme goal, and completely depend on Me. Always fix your mind on Me and resort to KarmaYog. (18.57) When your mind becomes fixed on Me, you shall overcome all difficulties by My grace. But, if you do not listen to Me due to ego, you shall perish. (18.58)

Karmic bondage and the free will

If due to ego you think: I shall not fight, your resolve is vain. Because, your own nature will compel you (to fight). (18.59) O Arjun, you are controlled by your own nature-born Karmic impressions (Samskaar). Therefore, you shall do—even against your will—what you do not wish to do out of delusion. (18.60) The Supreme Lord, abiding as the controller (Ishvar) in the causal heart (or the inner psyche) of all beings, O Arjun, causes them to act (or work out their Karm) like a puppet (of Karm) mounted on a machine. (18.61) Seek refuge in the Supreme Lord (Krishn or Ishvar) alone with loving devotion, O Arjun. By His grace you shall attain supreme peace and the Eternal Abode (ParamDhaam). (18.62) Thus, I have explained the knowledge that is more secret than the secret. After fully reflecting on this, do as you wish. (18.63)

Path of surrender is the ultimate path to God

Hear once again My most secret, supreme word. You are very dear to Me; therefore, I shall tell this for your benefit. (18.64) Fix your mind on Me, be devoted to Me, offer service to Me, bow down to Me, and you shall certainly reach Me. I promise you because you are My very dear friend. (18.65) Setting aside all meritorious deeds (Dharm), just surrender completely to My will (with firm faith and loving contemplation). I shall liberate you from all sins (or the bonds of Karm). Do not grieve. (18.66) (The meaning of abandoning all duties and taking refuge in the Lord is that one should perform duty without selfish attachment as an offering to the Lord, and totally depend only on the Him for help and guidance. The Lord takes full responsibility for a person who totally depends on Him with a spirit of genuine self-surrender.)

The highest service to God, and the best charity

This knowledge should never be spoken by you to one who is devoid of austerity, who is without devotion, who does not desire to listen, or who speaks ill of Me. (18.67) The one who shall propagate (or help the propagation of) this supreme secret philosophy (of the Gita) amongst My devotees, shall be performing the highest devotional service to Me and shall certainly (attain the Supreme Abode and) come to Me. (18.68) No other person shall do a more pleasing service to Me, and no one on the earth shall be more dear to Me. (18.69)

The grace of the Gita

Those who shall study our sacred dialogue shall be performing a holy act of sacrifice (JnaanYajn, knowledge-sacrifice). This is My promise. (18.70) Whoever hears or reads this sacred dialogue in the form of the Gita with faith and without cavil becomes free from sin, and attains heaven-the higher worlds of those whose actions are pure and virtuous. (18.71) O Arjun, did you listen to this with single-minded attention? Has your delusion born of ignorance been completely destroyed? (18.72)

Jainism

4.1 From the Kalpa Sutra: On the life of Mahavira

Then the Venerable Ascetic Mahavira-gazed on by a circle of thousands of eyes, praised by a circle of thousands of mouths, extolled by a circle of thousands of hearts, being the object of many thousands of wishes, desired because of his splendour, beauty, and virtues, pointed out by a circle of thousands of forefingers, answering with (a, salam) of his right hand a circle of thousands of joined hands of thousands of men and women, passing along -a row of thousands of palaces, greeted by sweet and delightful music, as beating of time, performance on the Vina, Turya, and the great drum, in which joined shouts of victory, and the low and pleasing murmur of the people; accompanied by all his pomp, all his splendour, all his army, all his train, by all his retinue- by all his magnificence, by all his grandeur, by all his ornaments, by all the tumult, by all the throng, by all subjects, by all actors, by all timebeaters, by the whole seraglio; adorned with flowers, scented robes, garlands, and ornaments, &c. which were accompanied at the same time by trumpets-went right through Kunda-pura to a park called the Shandavana of the Gñatris and proceeded to the excellent tree Asoka. There under the excellent tree Asoka he caused his palankin to stop, descended from his palankin, took off his ornaments, garlands, and finery with his own hands, and with his own bands plucked out his hair in five handfuls. When the moon was in conjunction with the asterism Uttaraphalguni, he, after fasting two and a half days' without drinking water, put on a divine robe, and quite alone, nobody else being present, he tore out his hair and leaving the house entered the state of houselessness.

The Venerable Ascetic Mahavira for a year anda month wore clothes; after that time he walked about naked, and accepted the alms in the hollow of his hand. For more than twelve years the Venerable Ascetic Mahivira neglected his body and abandoned the care of it; he with equanimity bore, underwent, and suffered all pleasant or unpleasant occurrences arising from divine powers, men, or animals.

Henceforth the Venerable Ascetic Mahavira was houseless, circumspect in his walking, circumspect in his speaking, circumspect in his begging, circumspect in his accepting (anything), in the carrying of his outfit and drinking vessel; circumspect in evacuating excrements, urine, saliva, mucus, and uncleanliness of the body; circumspect in his thoughts, circumspect in his words, circumspect in his acts; guarding his thoughts, guarding his words, guarding his acts, guarding his senses, guarding his chastity; without wrath, without pride, without deceit, without greed; calm, tranquil, composed, liberated, free from temptations, without egoism, without property; he had cut off all earthly ties, and was not stained by any worldliness: as water does not adhere to a copper vessel, or collyrium to mother of pearl (so sins found no place in him); his course was unobstructed like that of Life; like the firmament he wanted no support; like the wind he knew no obstacles; his heart was pure like the water (of rivers or tanks) in autumn; nothing could soil him like the leaf of a lotus; his senses were well protected like those of a tortoise; he was single and alone like the horn of a rhinoceros; he was free like a bird; he was always waking like the fabulous bird Bharundal, valorous like an elephant, strong like a bull, difficult to attack like a lion, steady and firm like Mount Mandara, deep like the ocean, mild like the moon, refulgent like the sun, pure like excellent gold'; like the earth he patiently bore everything; like a well-kindled fire he shone in his splendour.

These words have been summarized in two verses:

A vessel, mother of pearl, life, firmament, wind, water in autumn, leaf of lotus, a tortoise, a bird, a rhinoceros, and Bhirunda;

An elephant, a bull, a lion, the king of the mountains, and the ocean unshaken-tbe moon, the sun, gold, the earth, well-kindled fire.

There were no obstacles anywhere for the Venerable One. The obstacles have been declared to be of four kinds, viz. with regard to matter, space, time, affects. With regard to matter: in things animate, inanimate, and of a mixed state, with regard to space: in a village or a town or in a wood or in a field or a threshing-floor or a house' or a court-yard; with regard to time: in a Samayas or an Avalika or in the time of a respiration or in a Stoka or in a Kshana or in a Lava or in a Muhurta or in a day or in a fortnight or in a month or in a season or in a half year or in a year or in a long space of time; with regard to affects: in wrath or in pride or in deceit or in greed or in fear or in mirth or in love or in hate or in quarrelling or in calumny or in tale-bearing or in scandal or in pleasure or pain or in deceitful falsehood, &c. (all down to) or in the evil of wrong belief. There was nothing of this kind in the Venerable One.

The Venerable One lived, except in the rainy season, all the eight months of summer and winter, in villages only a single night, in towns only five nights; he was indifferent alike to the smell of ordure and of sandal, to straw and jewels, dirt and gold, pleasure and pain, attached neither to this world nor to that beyond, desiring neither life nor death, arrived at the other shore of the sams.Ara, and he exerted himself for the suppression of the defilement of Karman.

With supreme knowledge, with supreme intuition, with supreme conduct, in blameless lodgings, in blameless wandering, with supreme valour, with supreme uprightness, with supreme mildness, with supreme dexterity, with supreme patience, with supreme freedom from passions, with supreme control, with supreme contentment, with supreme understanding, on the supreme path to final liberation, which is the fruit of veracity, control, penance, and good conduct, the Venerable One meditated on himself for twelve years.

During the thirteenth year, in the second month of summer, in the fourth fortnight, the light (fortnight) of Vaisakha, on its tenth day, when the shadow had turned towards the east and the first wake was over, on the day called Suvrata, in the Muhurta called Vigaya, outside of the town Grimbhikagrama on the bank of the river Rigupalika, not far from an old temple, in the field of the householder Samaga, under a Sal tree, when the moon was in conjunction with the asterism Uttaraphalguni, (the Venerable One) in a squatting position with joined heels, exposing himself to the heat of the sun, after fasting two and a half days without drinking water, being engaged in deep meditation, reached the highest knowledge and intuition, called Kevala, which is infinite, supreme, unobstructed, unimpeded, complete, and full.

When the Venerable Ascetic Mahavira had become a Gina and Arhat, he was a Kevalin, omniscient and comprehending all objects; he knew and saw all conditions of the world, of gods, men, and demons: whence they come, whither they go, whether they are born as men or animals (kyavana) or become gods or hell-beings (upapada), the ideas, the thoughts of their minds, the food, doings, desires, the open and secret deeds of all the living beings in the whole world; he the Arhat, for whom there is no secret, knew and saw all conditions of all living beings in the world, what they thought, rpoke, or did at any moment.

In that period, in that age the Venerable Ascetic Mahavira stayed the first raimy season in Asthikagrama, three rainy seasons in Kampi and Prishtikampi, twelve in Vaisali and Vanigagrima, fourteen in Ragagriha and the suburbs of Nalanda, six in Mithila, two in Bhadrika, one in Alabhika, one in Panitabhumi one in Sravasti, one i.n the town of Papa in king Hastipala's office of the writers: that was his very last rainy season.

In the fourth month of that rainy season, in the seventh fortnight, in the dark (fortnight) of Karttika, on its fifteenth day, in the last night, in the town of Papa, in king Hastipala's office of the writers, the Venerable Ascetic Mahavira died, went off, quitted the world, cut asunder the ties of birth, old age, and death; became a Siddha, a Buddha, a Mukta, a maker of the end (to all misery), finally liberated, freed from all pains.

THE KALPA SUTRA OF BHADRABAHU.
LIVES OF THE GINAS. LIFE OF MAHAVIRA
http://www.sacred-texts.com/jai/kalpa.htm

4.2 From the Ankaranga Sutra: Begging for Food

When a male or a female mendicant, having entered the abode of a householder with the intention of collecting alms, recognises food, drink, dainties, and spices as affected by, or mixed up with, living beings, mildew, seeds or sprouts, or wet with water, or covered with dust-either in the hand or the pot of another-they should not, even if they can get it, accept of such food, thinking that it is impure and unacceptable.

But if perchance they accept of such food, under preising circumstances, they should go to a secluded spot, a garden, or a monk's hall-where there are no eggs, nor living beings, nor sprouts, nor dew, nor water, nor ants, nor mildew, nor drops (of water), nor mud, nor cobwebs-and rejecting (that which is affected by), and cleaning that which is mixed up (with living beings, &c.), they should circumspectly eat or drink it. But with what they cannot eat or drink, they should resort to a secluded spot, and leave it there on a heap of ashes or bones, or rusty things, or chaff, or cow-dung, or on any such-like place which they have repeatedly examined and cleaned.

A monk or a nun on a begging-tour should not accept as alms whatever herbs they recognise, on examining them, as still whole, containing their source of life, not split longwise or broadwise, and still alive, fresh beans, living and not broken; for such food is impure and unacceptable.

But when they recognise after examination that those herbs are no more whole, do not contain their source of life, are split longwise or broadwise, and no more alive, fresh beans, lifeless and broken, then they may accept them, if they get them; for they are pure and acceptable.

A monk or nun on a begging-tour should not accept as alms whatever flattened grains, grains containing much chaff, or half-roasted spikes of wheat, &c., or flour of wheat, &c., or rice or flour of rice, they recognise as only once worked [pounded or cooked or roasted, because after only one operation sperms of life might be left]; for such food is impure and unacceptable.

But when they recognise these things as more than once worked, as twice, thrice worked, then they may accept them, if they get them; for they are pure and acceptable.

A monk or a nun desiring to enter the abode of a householder for collecting alms, should not enter or leave it together with a heretic or a householder; or a monk who avoids all forbidden food, &c., together with one who does not.

A monk or a nun entering or leaving the out-of-door places for religious practices or for study should not do so together with a heretic or a householder; or a monk who avoids all forbidden food, together with one who does not.

A monk or a nun wandering from village to village should not do so together with a heretic or a householder; or a monk who avoids all forbidden food, together with one who does not.

A monk or a nun on a begging-tour should not give, immediately or mediately, food, &c., to a heretic or a householder; or a monk who avoids all forbidden food, to one who does not.

A monk or a nun on a begging-tour should not accept food, &c., from a householder whom they know to give out of respect for a Nirgrantha, in behalf of a fellow-ascetic, food, &c., which he has bought or stolen or taken, though it was not to be taken nor given, but was taken by force, by acting sinfully towards all sorts of living beings; for such-like food, &c., prepared by another man or by the giver himself, brought out of the house or not brought out of the house, belonging to the giver or not belonging to him, partaken or tasted of, or not partaken or tasted of, is impure and unacceptable.

In this precept substitute for 'on behalf of one fellow-ascetic,' on behalf of many fellow-ascetics, on behalf of one female fellow-ascetic, on behalf of many female fellow-ascetics; so that there will be four analogous precepts.

A monk or a nun should not accept of food, &c., which they know has been prepared by the householder for the sake of many Sramanas and Brahmanas, guests, paupers, and beggars, after he has counted them, acting sinfully towards all sorts of living beings; for such food, whether it be tasted of or not, is impure and unacceptable.

A monk or a nun should not accept of food, &c., procured in the way described in for the sake of the persons mentioned in, if the said food, &c., has been prepared by the giver himself, has been brought out of the house, does not belong to the giver, has not been partaken or tasted of; for such food, &c.,, is impure and unacceptable; but if the food, &c., has been prepared by another person, has been brought out of the house, belongs to the giver, has been partaken or tasted of, one may accept it; for it is pure and acceptable.

A monk or a nun wishing to enter the abode of a householder with the intention of collecting alms, should not, for the sake of food or drink, enter or leave such always liberal, always open houses, where they always give a morsel, always the best morsel, always a part of the meal, always nearly the half of it.

This certainly is the whole duty of a monk or a nun in which one should, instructed in all its meanings and endowed with bliss, always exert oneself.

Thus I say.

A monk or a nun on a begging-tour should not accept food, &c., in the following case: when, on the eighth or paushadha day, on the beginning of a fortnight, of a month, of two, three, four, five, or six months, or on the days of the seasons, of the junction of the seasons, of the intervals of the seasons, many Sramanas and Brahmanas, guests, paupers, and beggars are entertained with food, &c., out of one or two or three or four vessels, pots, baskets, or heaps of food; such-like food which has been prepared by the giver, &c., (all down to) not tasted of, is impure and unacceptable. But if it is prepared by another person, &c. (see first lesson, § 13), one may accept it; for it is pure and acceptable.

A monk or a nun on a begging-tour may accept food, &c., from unblamed, uncensured families, to wit, noble families, distinguished families, royal families, families belonging to the line of Ikshvaku, of Hari, cowherds' families, Vaisya families, barbers' families, carpenters' families, takurs' families, weavers' families; for such food, &c., is pure and acceptable.

A monk or a nun on a begging-tour should not accept food, &c., in the following case: when in assemblies, or during offerings to the manes, or on a festival of Indra or Skanda or Rudra or Mukunda or demons or Yakshas or the snakes, or on a festival in honour of a tomb, or a shrine, or a tree, or a hill, or a cave, or a well, or a tank, or a pond, or a river, or a lake, or the sea, or a mine-when on such-like various festivals many Sramanas and Brahmanas, guests, paupers, and beggars are entertained with food, &c. acceptable.

But when he perceives that all have received their due share, and are enjoying their meal, he should address the householder's wife or sister or daughter-in-law or nurse or male or female servant or slave and say: 'O long-lived one! (or, O sister!) will you give me something to eat?' After these words of the mendicant, the other may bring forth food, &c., and give it him. Such food, &c., whether he beg for it or the other give it, he may accept; for it is pure and acceptable.

When a monk or a nun knows that at a distance of more than half a yogana, a festive entertainment is going on, they should not resolve to go there for the sake of the festive entertainment.

SECOND BOOK FIRST PART FIRST LECTURE, CALLED BEGGING OF FOOD.
http://www.sacred-texts.com/jai/akaranga.htm

Buddhism

5.1 Theravada Buddhism

5.11 Selections from the Dhammapada

As rain penetrates
The poorly thatched dwelling,
So passion penetrates
The untended mind.

As rain does not penetrate
The well-thatched dwelling,
So passion does not penetrate
The well-tended mind.

If one, though reciting much of texts,
Is not a doer thereof, a heedless man;
He, like a cowherd counting others' cows,
Is not a partaker in the religious quest.

If one, though reciting little of texts,
Lives a life in accord with dhamma,
Having discarded passion, ill will, and
    unawareness,
Knowing full well, the mind well freed,

He, not grasping here, neither hereafter,
Is a partaker of the religious quest.

The path to the Deathless is awareness;
Unawareness, the path of death.
They who are aware do not die;
They who are unaware are as dead.

Among those unaware, the one aware,
Among the sleepers, the wide-awake,
The one with great wisdom moves on,
As a racehorse who leaves behind a nag.

Commendable is the taming
Of mind, which is hard to hold down,
Nimble, alighting wherever it wants.
Mind subdued brings ease.

Soon indeed
This body on the earth will lie,

Pitched aside, without consciousness,
Like a useless chip of wood.

Let one regard
Neither the discrepancies of others,
Nor what is done or left undone by
      others,
But only the things one has done oneself
      or left undone.

Long is the night for one awake,
Long is a league to one exhausted,
Long is samsara to the childish ones
Who know not dhamma true.

One who drinks of dhamma sleeps at
      ease,
With mind calmly clear.
In dhamma made known by noble
      ones,
The wise one constantly delights.

Even as a solid rock
Does not move on account of the wind,
So are the wise not shaken
In the face of blame and praise.

Even as a deep lake
Is very clear and undisturbed,
So do the wise become calm,
Having heard the words of dhamma.

Few are they among humans,
The people who reach the shore beyond.
But these other folk
Only run along the [hither] bank.

To one who has gone the distance,
Who is free of sorrows, freed in every
      respect;
To one who has left behind all bonds,
Fever there exists not.

He, truly, is supreme in battle,
Who would conquer himself alone,
Rather than he who would conquer in
      battle
A thousand, thousand men.

And should one live a hundred years
Indolent, of inferior enterprise;
Better still is one day lived
Of one initiating enterprise, firm.

Think not triflingly of wrong,
"It will not come to me!"
With falling drops of water,
Even a waterpot is filled.
A childish one is filled with wrong,
Acquiring bit by bit.

Think not triflingly of good,
"It will not come to me!"
With falling drops of water

That spot in the world is not found,
Neither in the sky nor in the ocean's
      depths,
Nor having entered into a cleft in moun-
      tains,
Where abiding, one would be released
      from the bad deed.

That spot one does not find,
Neither in the sky nor in the ocean's
      depths,
Nor having entered into a cleft in moun-
      tains,
Where abiding, death would not over-
      whelm one.

Quite wasted away is this form,
A nest for disease, perishable.
This putrid accumulation breaks up.
For life has its end in death.

By oneself is wrong done,
By oneself is one defiled.
By oneself wrong is not done,
By oneself, surely, is one cleansed.
One cannot purify another;
Purity and impurity are in oneself
    [alone].

Come ye, look at this world—
Like an adorned royal chariot—
Wherein childish ones are immersed;
No clinging there is among those who
    really know.

Many for refuge go
To mountains and to forests.
To shrines that are groves or trees—
Humans who are threatened by fear.

This is not a refuge secure,
This refuge is not the highest.
Having come to this refuge,
One is not released from all misery.

But who to the Buddha, Dhamma,
And Sangha as refuge has gone,
Sees with full insight
The four noble truths;

Misery, the arising of misery,
And the transcending of misery,
The noble Eightfold Path
Leading to the allaying of misery.

This, indeed, is a refuge secure.
This is the highest refuge.
Having come to this refuge,
One is released from all misery.

Hard to come by is a person of nobility;
Not everywhere is he born.
Wherever that wise one is born,
That family prospers in happiness.

Winning, one engenders enmity;
Miserably sleeps the defeated.
The one at peace sleeps pleasantly,
Having abandoned victory and defeat.

Like a yellow leaf are you now;
And even Yama's men have appeared
    for you;
And at the threshold of departure you
    stand;
But even the journey's provisions you do
    not have.

There is no fire like passion.
There is no grip like ill will.
There is no snare like delusion.
There is no river like craving.

One is not a learned one
Merely because one speaks much.
The one secure, without enmity, without
    fear,
Is called a "learned one."

That man of entangled mind,
Inebriated by sons and cattle,
Death carries away
Like a great flood, a sleeping village.

Excellent are tamed mules,
Thoroughbreds and horses of Sindh,
Also tuskers, great elephants.
But better than them is one who has sub-
    dued oneself.

The craving of a person who lives heed-
    lessly
Grows like a m?luv? creeper.
He moves from beyond to beyond,
Like a monkey, in a forest, wishing for
    fruit.

As long as the roots are unharmed, firm,

A tree, though topped, grows yet again.
Just so, when the latent craving is not
　　rooted out,
This suffering arises again and again.

Let go in front, let go behind, let go in
　　between!
Gone to the further shore of existence,
With mind released as to "everything,"
You shall not again come upon birth and
　　old age.

The gift of dhamma prevails over every
　　gift,
The flavor of dhamma prevails over
　　every flavor,
The delight in dhamma prevails over
　　every delight,
The dissolution of craving subdues all
　　suffering.

5.12　Selections from the Discourse on the Analysis of the Undefiled

THUS have I heard: At one time the Lord was staying near S?vatthï in the Jeta Grove in An?thapindika's monastery. While he was there the Lord addressed the monks, saying: "Monks." "Revered One," these monks answered the Lord in assent. The Lord spoke thus: "I will teach you, monks, the analysis of the undefiled. Listen carefully to it, pay attention and I will speak." "Yes, revered sir," these monks answered the Lord in assent. The Lord spoke thus:

"You should not be intent on the happiness of sense-pleasures which is low, of the villager, of the average person, unariyan, not connected with the goal; nor should you be intent on the practice, of self-mortification which is sorrowful, unariyan, not connected with the goal. Not approaching either of these two dead-ends, there is the Middle Course awakened to by the Tath?gata, making for vision, making for knowledge, and conducing to calm, super-knowledge, self-awakening and nibb?na. One should know approval and one should know disapproval, and having known approval, having known disapproval, one should neither approve nor disapprove-one should simply teach *dhamma*. One should know how to judge what happiness is; having known how to judge what happiness is, one should be intent on inward happiness. One should not utter a secret speech, face to face (with a man) one should not tell (him) a vexatious thing. One should speak quite slowly, not hurriedly. One should not affect the dialect of the countryside, one should not deviate from recognised parlance. This is the exposition of the analysis of the undefiled.

When it is said, 'You should not be intent on the happiness of sense-pleasures ... nor should you be intent on the practice of self-mortification which is sorrowful, unariyan, not connected with the goal,' in reference to what is it said? Whatever is happiness in association with sense-pleasures and intentness on a joy that is low, of the villager, of the average man, unariyan, not connected with the goal-this is a thing that has anguish, annoyance, trouble and fret; it is a wrong course. But whatever is happiness in association with sense-pleasures but not intentness on a joy that is low, of the villager ... not connected with the goal-this is a thing without anguish, annoyance, trouble or fret; it is the right course. Whatever is intentness on self-mortification which is sorrowful, unariyan, not connected with the goal-this is a thing that has anguish, annoyance, trouble and fret; it is a wrong course. But whatever is non-intentness on self-mortification which is sorrowful, unariyan, not connected with the goal-this is a thing without anguish, annoyance, trouble or fret; it is the right course. When it is said, 'You should not be intent on the happiness of sense-pleasures ... nor should you be intent on the practice of self-mortification which is sorrowful, unariyan, not connected with the goal,' it is said in reference to this.

When it is said, 'Not approaching either of these two dead-ends, there is the Middle Course awakened to by the Tath?gata, making for vision, making for knowledge, that conduces to calm, super-knowledge, self-awakening and nibb?na,' in reference to what is it said? It is the ariyan Eightfold Way itself, that is to say: right view, right aspiration, right speech, right action, right mode of livelihood, right endeavour, right mindfulness, right concentration. When it is said, 'Not approaching either of these two dead-ends, there is the Middle Course ... that conduces to ... nibb?na,' it is said in reference to this.

When it is said, 'One should know approval and one should know disapproval, and having known approval, having known disapproval, one should neither approve nor disapprove-one should simply teach *dhamma*,' in reference to what is it said?

And what, monks, is approval and what is disapproval but not the teaching of *dhamma*? He disapproves of some (people) here, saying: 'All those who find happiness in association with sense-pleasures and are intent on a joy that is low, of the villager, of the average man, unariyan, not connected with the goal, have anguish, annoyance, trouble and fret; they are faring along wrongly.' He approves of some (people) here, saying: 'All those who find happiness in association with sense-pleasures but are not intent on a joy that is low ... not connected with the goal, are without anguish, annoyance, trouble or fret; they are faring along rightly.' He disapproves of some (people) here, saying: 'All those who are intent on the practice of self-mortification, which is sorrowful, unaryian, not connected with the goal, have anguish, annoyance, trouble and fret; they are faring along wrongly.' He approves of some (people) here, saying: 'All those who are not intent on the practice of self-mortification, which is sorrowful, unariyan, not connected with the goal, are without anguish, annoyance, trouble or fret; they are faring along rightly.' He disapproves of some (people) here, saying: 'All those in whom the fetter of becoming is not got rid of have anguish, annoyance, troble and fret; they are faring along wrongly.' He approves of some (people) here, saying: 'All those in whom the fetter of becoming is got rid of are without anguish, annoyance, trouble or fret; they are faring along rightly.' This, monks, is what is approval and disapproval but not the teaching of *dhamma*.

And what, monks, is neither approval nor disapproval, but the teaching of *dhamma*? He does not speak thus: 'All those who find happiness in association with sense-pleasures and are intent on a joy that is low, of the villager, of the average man, unariyan, not connected with the goal, have anguish, annoyance, trouble and fret; they are faring along wrongly.' He simply teaches *dhamma*, saying: 'Intentness is a thing that has anguish, annoyance, trouble and fret; it is a wrong course.' He does not speak thus: 'All those who find happiness in association with sense-pleasures but are not intent on a joy that is low ... not connected with the goal, are without anguish, annoyance, trouble or fret; they are faring along rightly.' He simply teaches *dhamma*, saying: 'Non-intentness is a thing that is without anguish, annoyance, trouble or fret; it is the right course.' He does not speak thus: 'All those who are intent on the practice of self-mortification which is sorrowful, unariyan, not connected with the goal, have anguish, annoyance, trouble and fret; they are faring along wrongly.' He simply teaches *dhamma*, saying: 'Intentness is a thing that has anguish ... fret; it is a wrong course.' He does not speak thus: 'All those who are not intent on the practice of self-mortification ... are without anguish ... fret; they are faring along rightly.' He simply teaches *dhamma*, saying: 'Non-intentness is a thing that is without anguish ... fret; it is the right course.' He does not speak thus: 'All those in whom the fetter of becoming is not got rid of have anguish, annoyance, trouble and fret; they are faring along wrongly.' He simply teaches *dhamma*, saying: 'While the fetter of becoming is not got rid of, becoming is not got rid of.' He does not speak thus: 'All those in whom the fetter of becoming is got rid of are without anguish ... fret; they are faring along rightly.' He simply teaches *dhamma*, saying: 'If the fetter of becoming is got rid of, becoming is got rid of.' This, monks, is what is neither approval nor disapproval, but the teaching of *dhamma*. When it is said: 'One should know approval and one should know disapproval, and having known approval, having known disapproval, one should neither approve nor disapprove-one should simply teach *dhamma*,' it is said in reference to this.

When it is said: 'One should know how to judge what happiness is; having known how to judge what happiness is, one should be intent on inward happiness,' in reference to what is it said? These five, monks, are the strands of sense-pleasures. What five? Material shapes cognisable by the eye ... sounds cognisable by the ear ... smells cognisable by the nose ... tastes cognisable by the tongue ... touches cognisable by the body, agreeable, pleasant, liked, enticing, connected with sensual pleasure, alluring. These, monks, are the five strands of sense-pleasures. Whatever happiness or joy, monks, arises in consequence of these five strands of sense-pleasures is said to be a happiness of sense-pleasures, a vile happiness, the happiness of an average person, an unariyan happiness. I say of this happiness that it is not to be pursued, developed or made much of-it is to be feared. As to this, monks, a monk, aloof from pleasures of the senses, aloof from unskilled states of mind, enters on and abides in the first meditation ... the second ... the third ... the fourth meditation. This is said to be the happiness of renunciation, the happiness of aloofness, the happiness of tranquillity, the happiness of self-awakening. I say of this happiness that it is to be pursued, developed and made much of-it is not to be feared.

5.13 A Thai Buddhist Sermon

Once upon a time, when the Lord Buddha was alive and was living at the great temple of We-ruwan, which was built to be presented to the Lord Buddha by Phraja-Phimphisa-n, there was a monk among his disciples, whose name was Sa-raphud The-ra-, who loved to stay in the deep jungle. One day the monk asked leave of the Lord Buddha and went away to stay in the jungle near the village Pacanthakha-m. The monk lived under a huge banyan tree and spent his time studying the Law of Buddha. In a nearby village there lived a hunter who was very poor. He had to hunt animals and sell them to the villagers in order to make money for his livelihood. One day, as he was hunting, he passed the place where the Sa-raphud The-ra- was residing. When the hunter noticed the handsome monk and became aware of his clear mind, he was at once attracted to him. He sat down in a befitting place and asked the monk:

"Oh, my most respected monk! I am a poor man who has to earn his living by killing animals. This is wrong according to the Law of the Lord Buddha, and I have, therefore, sinned very much. How can I find a trustworthy way to earn my living without sinning? Please, my most respected monk, kindly lead me to find that way."

The monk knew that the hunter was an impious man. So he said, "Listen to me, hunter. If you want to find bliss without sin for the rest of your life in this world and new life in the other world, you must keep the Trinity for your support; and you must keep the five precepts in your mind. The power to keep the precepts will bring you the best merit."

The hunter then asked the monk to explain the meaning of the Trinity and of the five precepts.

"Listen to me," said the monk; "the Trinity is composed of the Lord Buddha, the Law of Buddha, and the Monkhood, who are the disciples of the Lord Buddha.

"The five precepts are:

do not destroy life,
do not covet another's property,
do not commit adultery,
do not deceive, and
do not partake of intoxicants."

"What results does one achieve who keeps the five precepts and pays respect to the Trinity?" asked the hunter.

The monk answered, "Listen to me, hunter. He who pays most reverend respect to the Trinity and keeps the five precepts firmly in his mind will never be reborn as follows:

1. in *narog* (i.e., in hell),
2. as a *pre-d* (i.e., as the ghost of an evil-doer),
3. as a haunting spirit, or
4. as an animal.

"But such people will go to a good place called *sawan*. If they have accumulated very much merit, they will encounter the path leading away from evil-doing and reach eternal peace, which *phra nibpha-n*" (*nirvana*).

After listening appreciatively to all of this, the hunter promised to keep the Trinity and the five precepts as his paradigms. Upon returning to his house, the hunter told his wife that he was keeping the most respected precepts given him by a monk he had met in the jungle, and that from then on he would not kill any living thing according to these precepts.

The wife became very angry with her husband, the hunter, and so reproved him for what he had done. She told him to return the precepts to the monk who had given them to him. The hunter restrained himself for seven days until he lost patience and ga... in to his wife because of her constant nagging. He agreed... return the precepts to the monk according to his wife's wishes. He then went to the place where he first had met the monk.

When the hunter arrived at the place where the monk Sa-raphud was staying, he prostrated himself three times and requested to be permitted to return the five precepts. However, Phra Sa-raphud would not accept them. He said that the precepts belonged to the Lord Buddha, who was the only one who could receive them back.

The hunter acknowledged the words of the monk and proceeded to the place where the Lord Buddha was staying. On his way to the Lord Buddha, the hunter encountered five strange events:

1. He met a king whose city was damaged by fire once every year until the king could no longer stay in his palace. The king requested the hunter to ask the Lord Buddha the reason for the fire, and to bring the answer back to him when he returned.
2. He met a big boa constrictor that was living in an anthill, unable to move to any other place. The boa wanted to know from the Lord Buddha why he could not move anywhere else.
3. He met five hundred naked *na-ng pre-d* (female ghost) who had plenty of food to eat. The *na-ng pre-d*'s duty was to guard a hill; they were not able to go to any other place. The *na-ng pre-d* wanted to know from the Lord Buddha why they were in this condition.
4. He met a white elephant living in a bamboo jungle. The white elephant wanted to know from the Lord Buddha why he had to stay in a place like that where he had only bamboo to eat.
5. He met one thousand drunken *pre-d* (male ghosts) who had lost their senses and were fighting for seven days to kill each other. They recovered on the eighth day and stopped fighting to have some rest and feed themselves. On the next day they would start fighting again for seven days and stop on the eighth, and so on. The *pre-d* wanted to know from the Lord Buddha what caused their peculiar behavior.

The hunter remembered all these stories and proceeded to the place where the Lord Buddha was staying. At the time of the hunter's arrival, the Lord Buddha was preaching to the faithful. So the hunter joined the people listening to the preaching.

Through the holy power of the preaching of the Lord Buddha, faith grew in the mind of the hunter until he gave up his plan to return the five precepts to the Lord Buddha. To the contrary, he became more firmly attached in his mind to the teachings of the Buddha.

When the Lord Buddha had finished his sermon, the hunter went to see him. He prostrated himself three times and presented him with a bunch of lotus blossoms. Then he related the stories which he had been asked to tell the Lord Buddha. The Lord Buddha listened carefully to all the stories and then delivered the following answers:

The king, whose city was damaged by fire once every year, had been a wood cutter in his former life and had always set fire to the jungle. Through the power of his good deeds of offering food to the monks every Precept Day, he was reborn as king in this life, but his city caught fire once a year, because of the vicious sin of burning the jungle in his former life.

The boa was a rich man in his former life, whose wealth totaled about 800 million *baht*. He had been miserly and never made any merit. When the rich man had fallen seriously ill, he had hidden gold worth some twenty thousand *baht* in an anthill. When he died, he was reborn as a boa to guard his wealth in the anthill.

The five hundred *na-ng pre-d* were pig-raising girls in their former lives, who raised pigs for sale in the market and spent the money on food and clothing for themselves. On every Precept Day, these pig-raising women made merit in the temple and kept the eight precepts. When they died, they were reborn in hell for three thousand years because of their vicious sin of selling pigs. Then they were reborn as *na-ng pre-d* and sent to guard the hill. They were wearing no clothes because they had sold the pigs to buy clothing. They had food because they had made merit every Precept Day and had kept the eight precepts.

The white elephant had been an unjust judge in his former life and had always worked with four biases:

- the bias of favoritism,
- the bias of temper,
- the bias of fear, and
- the bias of passion.

After his death the unjust judge was reborn as a white elephant and confined to the bamboo jungle because of his vicious sins.

The thousand drunken *pre-d* were gamblers and drunkards in their former lives, who had drunk and gambled every day. They had stopped only on Precept Day to go to the temple to make merit. When they died, they were reborn in hell for a very long time. From hell they were reborn as *pre-d* fighting each other for seven days, stopping only on the eighth. They stopped fighting and received food on that day because of the merit they had made going to the temple every Precept Day.

The hunter remembered all the answers and went back to tell those concerned what he had heard. When all of the *na-ng pre-d*, the boa, and the drunken *pre-d*, heard the answers brought to them by the hunter, they were very happy and submitted themselves to be the hunter's slaves.

He told them, however, to remain at the places where they had been for the time being. Then the hunter proceeded to meet the king of the burning city and told him what he had heard from the Lord Buddha. The king rejoiced greatly, granted the hunter his daughter as his wife, and appointed him Phra Sin Sa-ra Ra-dcha Bud. Phra Sin Sa-ra showed his might by calling the one thousand *pre-d* to be his soldiers, the *na-ng pre-d* to be his servants, and the white elephant to be his beast of burden. He brought twenty thousand *baht* worth of gold, part of the wealth of the boa, to the city. The king told all the people in the city to hold a month-long fair to celebrate the new Phra Sin Sa-ra. After that, fire never again occurred in the city, and the people lived happily ever after.

A year later the king died, and Phra Sin Sa-ra became king of the city. The new king sent his men to tell everybody to keep the five or eight precepts and to make merit often.

Once there were one thousand monks who had traveled from other countries and asked the king for food. He told his servants to offer food to all the monks and invite them to stay in his palace.

The monks accepted the king's invitation and stayed in the palace for four months. Then they left and presented themselves to the Lord Buddha at Maha- Wiha-n Sa-wadthi-. There they asked the Lord Buddha to tell them the story of Phra Sin Sa-ra.

The Lord Buddha told the story of Phra Sin Sa-ra to the one thousand monks and preached about the value of keeping the precepts. Every man and woman who can keep the precepts in mind will attain *nibpha-n* in a future life. Such a person will also receive three kinds of property, which are:

> human property,
> heavenly property, and
> *nibpha-n* property.

The precepts are the roots of religion. A religion can remain alive so long as there is someone who keeps the precepts. The precepts are the most important aspects of religion.

The one thousand monks accepted the lesson from the Lord Buddha, paid their respects, and went back to their own countries.

Phra Sin Sa-ra had been on the throne of the country for about twenty years when the white elephant died. Phra Sin Sa-ra was miserable because of the elephant's death. He thought that all living things must die in the end.

He then desired to become a monk to keep his chastity for *phra nibpha-n*. He, therefore, called his son, turned over his throne to him, and taught him to govern the city morally.

Phra Sin Sa-ra then went to the Lord Buddha and requested his permission to become a monk. The Lord Buddha granted his wish and named him Phra Sin Sa-ra

The-ra-. Phra Sin Sa-ra The-ra- spent all of his time studying the Law of Buddha until he found the way to be Phra Arahad.

All the other monks, including Phra A-non, approached the Lord Buddha to ask him, "My dear Lord Buddha, who is always growing in mind, who is very kind to the creatures in the three worlds, who is teaching the creatures about heaven and *nibpha-n* to lead them away from *o-khakanda-n*-the wandering life-we want to know of you, Lord Buddha, who will take your place teaching the people when you die? Who will be preaching to the creatures?"

The Lord Buddha answered, "When I, Tatha-khod, attain *nibpha-n*, all the creatures will lose faith in religion. They will not learn or remember what I have said. The clergy will abandon their precepts; they will only desire to sin. The laity will not follow the five precepts, either; they will not think of their future life. But see, A-non, men or women who are in company with learned people, who always follow the precepts, will receive permanent happiness, such as the crude hunter received, who joined wise men and accepted the five precepts as a beginning to doing good, and by his later good deeds, such as making merit, helped himself to attain *nibpha-n* in the end."

When the Lord Buddha had finished preaching, all the creatures that had listened received merit from the preaching according to the attention they had paid. For what is said in the Law of Buddha is all preached.

5.2 Mahayana Buddism

5.21 The Bodhisattva

Please listen with all of your attention and the Tathágata will respond to your question. If daughters and sons of good families want to give rise to the highest, most fulfilled, awakened mind, they should rely on the following way."

The Venerable Subhuti said, "Lord, we are so happy to hear your teachings."

The Buddha said to Subhuti, "This is how the bodhisattva Mahasattvas master their thinking. 'However many species of living beings there are—whether born from eggs, from the womb, from moisture, or spontaneously; whether they have form or do not have form; whether they have perceptions or do not have perceptions; or whether it cannot be said of them that they have perceptions or that they do not have perceptions, we must lead all these beings to the ultimate nirvana so that they can be liberated. And when this innumerable, immeasurable, infinite number of beings has become liberated, we do not, in truth, think that a single being has been liberated,'

"Why is this so? If, Subhuti, a bodhisattva holds on to the idea that a self, a person, a living being, or a life span exists, that person is not an authentic bodhisattva."

"Moreover, Subhuti, when a bodhisattva practices generosity, he does not rely on any object—that is to say he does not rely on any form, sound, smell, taste, tactile object, or dharma—to practice generosity. That, Subhuti, is the spirit in which a bodhisattva should practice generosity, not relying on signs. Why? If a bodhisattva practices generosity without relying on signs, the happiness that results cannot be conceived of or measured. Subhuti, do you think that the space in the Eastern Quarter can be measured?"

"No, World-Honored One."

"Subhuti, can space in the Western, Southern, and Northern Quarters, above and below be measured?"

"No, World-Honored One."

"Subhuti, if a bodhisattva does not rely on any concept when practicing generosity, then the happiness that results from that virtuous act is as great as space. It cannot be measured. Subhuti, the bodhisattvas should let their minds dwell in the teachings I have just given."

"What do you think, Subhuti? Is it possible to grasp the Tathágata by means of bodily signs?"

"No, World-Honored One. When the Tathágata speaks of bodily signs, there are no signs being talked about."

The Buddha said to Subhuti: "In a place where there is something that can be distinguished by signs, in that place there is deception. If you can see the signless nature of signs, then you can see the Tathágata."

The Venerable Subhuti said to the Buddha, "In times to come, will there be people who, when they hear these teachings, have real faith and confidence in them?"

The Buddha replied, "Do not speak that way, Subhuti. Five hundred years after the Tathágata has passed away, there will still be people who enjoy the happiness that comes from observing the precepts. When such people hear these words, they will have faith and confidence that here is the truth. We should know that such people have sown seeds not only during the lifetime of one Buddha, or even two, three, four, or five Buddhas, but have, in truth, planted wholesome seeds during the lifetimes of tens of thousands of Buddhas. Anyone who, for only a second, gives rise to a pure and clear confidence upon hearing these words of the Tathágata, the Tathágata sees and knows that person, and he or she will attain immeasurable happiness because of this understanding. Why?

"Because that kind of person is not caught up in the idea of a self, a person, a living being, or a life span. They are not caught up in the idea of a dharma or the idea of a non-dharma. They are not caught up in the notion that this is a sign and that is not a sign. Why? If you are caught up in the idea of a dharma, you are also caught up in the ideas of a self, a person, a living being, and a life span. If you are caught up in the idea that there is no dharma, you are still caught up in the ideas of a self, a person, a living being, and a life span. That is why we should not get caught up in dharmas or in the idea that dharmas do not exist. This is the hidden meaning when the Tathágata says, 'Bhikshus, you should know that all of the teachings I give to you are a raft.? All teachings must be abandoned, not to mention non-teachings."

"What do you think, Subhuti, has the Tathágata arrived at the highest, most fulfilled, awakened mind? Does the Tathágata give any teaching?"

The Venerable Subhuti replied, "As far as I have understood the Lord Buddha's teachings, there is no independently existing object of mind called the highest, most fulfilled, awakened mind, nor is there any independently existing teaching that the Tathágata gives. Why? The teachings that the Tathágata has realized and spoken of cannot be conceived of as separate, independent existences and therefore cannot be described. The Tathágatas teaching is not self-existent nor is it non-self-existent. Why? Because the noble teachers are only distinguished from others in terms of the unconditioned."

"What do you think, Subhuti? If someone were to fill the 3,000 chiliocosms with the seven precious treasures as an act of generosity, would that person bring much happiness by this virtuous act?"

The Venerable Subhuti replied, "Yes, World-Honored One. It is because the very natures of virtue and happiness are not virtue and happiness that the Tathágata is able to speak about virtue and happiness."

The Buddha said, "On the other hand, if there is someone who accepts these teachings and puts them into practice, even if only a gatha of four lines, and explains them to someone else, the happiness brought about by this virtuous act far exceeds the happiness brought about by giving the seven precious treasures. Why? Because, Subhuti, all Buddhas and the dharma of the highest, most fulfilled, awakened mind of all Buddhas arise from these teachings. Subhuti, what is called Buddha dharma is everything that is not Buddha dharma."

"What do you think, Subhuti? Does a Stream-Enterer think, 'I have attained the fruit of stream-entry.'?"

Subhuti replied, "No, World-Honored One. Why? Stream-Enterer means to enter the stream, but in fact there is no stream to enter. One does not enter a stream that is form, nor a stream that is sound, smell, taste, touch, or object of mind. That is what we mean when we say entering a stream."

"What do you think, Subhuti? Does a Once-Returner think, 'I have attained the fruit of Once-Returning.'?"

Subhuti replied, "No, World-Honored One. Why? Once-Returner means to go and return once more, but in truth there is no going just as there is no returning. That is what we mean when we say Once-Returner."

"What do you think, Subhuti? Does a Non-Returner think like this, 'I have attained the fruit of No-Return.'?"

Subhuti replied, "No, World-Honored One. Why? No-Return means not to return to this world, but in fact there cannot be any Non-Returning. That is what we mean when we say Non-Returner."

"What do you think, Subhuti? Does an Arhat think like this, 'I have attained the fruit of Arhatship??"

Subhuti replied, "No, World-Honored One. Why? There is no separately existing thing that can be called Arhat. If an Arhat gives rise to the thought that he has attained the fruit of Arhat-ship, then he is still caught up in the idea of a self, a person, a living being, and a life span. World-Honored One, you have often said that I have attained the concentration of peaceful abiding and that in the community, I am the Arhat who has most transformed need and desire. World-Honored One, if I were to think that I had attained the fruit of Arhat-ship, you certainly would not have said that I love to dwell in the concentration of peaceful abiding."

The Buddha asked Subhuti, "In ancient times when the Tathágata practiced under Buddha Dipankara, did he attain anything?"

Subhuti answered, "No, World-Honored One. In ancient times when the Tathágata was practicing under Buddha Dipankara, he did not attain anything."

"What do you think, Subhuti? Does a bodhisattva create a serene and beautiful Buddha field?"

"No, World-Honored One. Why? To create a serene and beautiful Buddha field is not in fact creating a serene and beautiful Buddha field. That is why it is called creating a serene and beautiful Buddha field."

The Buddha said, "So, Subhuti, all the bodhisattva Mahasattvas should give rise to a pure and clear intention in this spirit. When they give rise to this intention, they should not rely on forms, sounds, smells, tastes, tactile objects, or objects of mind. They should give rise to an intention with their minds not dwelling anywhere.'

"Subhuti, if there were someone with a body as big as Mount Sumeru, would you say that his was a large body?"

Subhuti answered, "Yes, World-Honored One, very large. Why? What the Tathágata says is not a large body, that is known as a large body."

"Subhuti, if there were as many Ganges Rivers as the number of grains of sand in the Ganges, would you say that the number of grains of sand in all those Ganges Rivers is very many'"

Subhuti answered, "Very many indeed, World-Honored One. If the number of Ganges Rivers were huge, how much more so the number of grains of sand in all those Ganges Rivers."

"Subhuti, now I want to ask you this: if a daughter or son of good family were to fill the 3,000 chiliocosms with as many precious jewels as the number of grains of sand in all the Ganges Rivers as an act of generosity, would that person bring much happiness by her virtuous act?"

Subhuti replied, "Very much, World-Honored One."

The Buddha said to Subhuti, "If a daughter or son of a good family knows how to accept, practice, and explain this sutra to others, even if it is a gatha of four lines, the happiness that results from this virtuous act would be far greater."

"Furthermore, Subhuti, any plot of land on which this sutra is proclaimed, even if only one gatha of four lines, will be a land where gods, men, and asuras will come to make offerings just as they make offerings to a stupa of the Buddha. If the plot of land is regarded as that sacred, how much more so the person who practices and recites this sutra. Subhuti, you should know that that person attains something rare and profound. Wherever this sutra is kept is a sacred site enshrining the presence of the Buddha or one of the Buddha's great disciples."

After that, Subhuti asked the Buddha, "What should this sutra be called and how should we act regarding its teachings?"

The Buddha replied, "This sutra should be called *The Diamond that Cuts through Illusion* because it has the capacity to cut through allusions and afflictions and bring us to the shore of liberation. Please use this title and practice according to its deepest meaning. Why? What the Tathágata has called the highest, transcendent understanding is not, in fact, the highest, transcendent understanding. That is why it is truly the highest, transcendent understanding:"

The Buddha asked, "What do you think, Subhuti? Is there any dharma that the Tathágata teaches?"

Subhuti replied, "The Tathágata has nothing to teach, World-Honored One."

"What do you think, Subhuti? Are there many particles of dust in the 3,000 chiliocosms?"

"Very many, World-Honored One."

"Subhuti, the Tathágata says that these particles of dust are not particles of dust, That is why they are truly particles of dust. And what the Tathágata calls chiliocosms are not in fact chiliocosms. That is why they are called chiliocosms"

"What do you think, Subhuti? Can the Tathágata be recognized by the possession of the thirty-two marks?"

The Venerable Subhuti replied, "No, World-Honored One. Why? Because what the Tathágata calls the thirty-two marks are not essentially marks and that is why the Tathágata calls them the thirty-two marks."

"Subhuti, if as many times as there are grains of sand in the Ganges a son or daughter of a good family gives up his or her life as an act of generosity and if another daughter or son of a good family knows how to accept, practice, and explain this sutra to others, even if only a gatha of four lines, the happiness resulting from explaining this sutra is far greater."

When he had heard this much and penetrated deeply into its significance, the Venerable Subhuti was moved to tears. He said, "World-Honored One, you are truly rare in this world. Since the day I attained the eyes of understanding, thanks to the guidance of the Buddha, I have never before heard teachings so deep and wonderful as these. World-Honored One, if someone hears this sutra, has pure and clear confidence in it, and arrives at insight into the truth, that person will realize the rarest kind of virtue. World-Honored One, that insight into the truth is essentially not insight. That is what the Tathágata calls insight into the truth.

"World-Honored One, today it is not difficult for me to hear this wonderful sutra, have confidence in it, understand it, accept it, and put it into practice. But in the future, in 500 years, if there is someone who can hear this sutra, have confidence in it, understand it, accept it, and put it into practice, then certainly the existence of someone like that will be great and rare. Why? That person will not be dominated by the idea of a self, a person, a living being, or a life span. Why? The idea of a self is not an idea, and the ideas of a person, a living being, and a life span are not ideas either. Why? Buddhas are called Buddhas because they are free of ideas."

"The Buddha said to Subhuti, "That is quite right. If someone hears this sutra and is not terrified or afraid, he or she is rare. Why? Subhuti, what the Tathágata calls parama-paramita, the highest transcendence, is not essentially the highest transcendence, and that is why it is called the highest transcendence.

"Subhuti, the Tathágata has said that what is called transcendent endurance is not transcendent endurance. That is why it is called transcendent endurance. Why? Subhuti, thousands of lifetimes ago when my body was cut into pieces by King Kalinga, I was not caught in the idea of a self, a person, a living being, or a life span. If, at that time, I had been caught up in any of those ideas, I would have felt anger and ill-will against the king.

"I also remember in ancient times, for 500 lifetimes, I practiced transcendent endurance by not being caught up in the idea of a self, a person, a living being, or a life span. So, Subhuti, when a bodhisattva gives rise to the unequalled mind of awakening, he has to give up all ideas. He cannot not rely on forms when he gives rise to that mind, nor on sounds, smells, tastes, tactile objects, or objects of mind. He can only give rise to that mind that is not caught up in anything.

"The Tathágata has said that all notions are not notions and that all living beings are not living beings. Subhuti, the Tathágata is one who speaks of things as they are, speaks what is true, and speaks in accord with reality. He does not speak deceptively or to please people. Subhuti, if we say that the Tathágata has realized a teaching, that teaching is neither graspable nor deceptive.

"Subhuti, a bodhisattva who still depends on notions to practice generosity is like someone walking in the dark. He will not see anything. But when a bodhisattva does not depend on notions to practice generosity, he is like someone with good eyesight walking under the bright light of the sun. He can see all shapes and colors.

"Subhuti, if in the future there is any daughter or son of good family who has the capacity to accept, read, and put into practice this sutra, the Tathágata will see that person with his eyes of understanding. The Tathágata will know that person, and that person will realize the measureless, limitless fruit of her or his virtuous act.

"Subhuti, if on the one hand, a daughter or son of a good family gives up her or his life in the morning as many times as there are grains of sand in the Ganges as an act of generosity, and gives as many again in the afternoon and as many again in the evening, and continues doing so for countless ages; and if, on the other hand, another person listens to this sutra with complete confidence and without contention, that person's happiness will be far greater. But the happiness of one who writes this sutra down, receives, recites, and explains it to others cannot be compared.

"In summary, Subhuti, this sutra brings about boundless virtue and happiness that cannot be conceived or measured. If there is someone capable of receiving, practicing, reciting, and sharing this sutra with others, the Tathágata will see and know that person, and he or she will have inconceivable, indescribable, and incomparable virtue. Such a person will be able to shoulder the highest, most fulfilled, awakened career of the Tathágata. Why? Subhuti, if one is content with the small teachings, if he or she is still caught up in the idea of a self, a person, a living being, or a life span, he or she will not be able to listen, receive, recite, and explain this sutra to others. Subhuti, any place this sutra is found is a place where gods, men, and asuras will come to make offerings. Such a place is a shrine and should be venerated with formal ceremonies, circumambulations, and offerings of flowers and incense."

"Furthermore, Subhuti, if a son or daughter of good family, while reciting and practicing this sutra, is disdained or slandered, his or her misdeeds committed in past lives, including those that could bring about an evil destiny, will be eradicated, and he or she will attain the fruit of the most fulfilled, awakened mind. Subhuti, in ancient times before I met Buddha Dipankara, I had made offerings to and had been attendant of all 84,000 multi-millions of Buddhas. If someone is able to receive, recite, study, and practice this sutra in the last epoch, the happiness brought about by this virtuous act is hundreds of thousands times greater than that which I brought about in ancient times. In fact, such happiness cannot be conceived or compared with anything, even mathematically. Such happiness is immeasurable.

"Subhuti, the happiness resulting from the virtuous act of a son or daughter of good family who receives, recites, studies, and practices this sutra in the last epoch will be so great that if I were to explain it now in detail, some people would become suspicious and disbelieving, and their minds might become disoriented. Subhuti, you should know that the meaning of this sutra is beyond conception and discussion. Likewise, the fruit resulting from receiving and practicing this sutra is beyond conception and discussion."

At that time, the Venerable Subhuti said to the Buddha, "World-Honored One, may I ask you again that if daughters or sons of good family want to give rise to the highest, most fulfilled, awakened mind, what should they rely on and what should they do to master their thinking?"

The Buddha replied, "Subhuti, a good son or daughter who wants to give rise to the highest, most fulfilled, awakened mind should do it in this way: 'We must lead all beings to the shore of awakening, but, after these beings have become liberated, we do not, in truth, think that a single being has been liberated.' Why is this so? Subhuti, if a bodhisattva is still caught up in the idea of

a self, a person, a living being or a life span, that person is not an authentic bodhisattva. Why is that?

"Subhuti, in fact, there is no independently existing object of mind called the highest, most fulfilled, awakened mind. What do you think, Subhuti? In ancient times, when the Tathágata was living with Buddha Dipankara, did he attain anything called the highest, most fulfilled, awakened mind?"

"No, World-Honored One. According to what I understand from the teachings of the Buddha, there is no attaining of anything called the highest, most fulfilled, awakened mind."

The Buddha said, "Right you are, Subhuti. In fact, there does not exist the so-called highest, most fulfilled, awakened mind that the Tathágata attains. Because if there had been any such thing, Buddha Dipankara would not have predicted of me, 'In the future, you will come to be a Buddha called Shakyamuni.' This prediction was made because there is, in fact, nothing that can be attained that is called the highest, most fulfilled, awakened mind. Why? Tathágata means the such-ness of all things (dharmas). Someone would be mistaken to say that the Tathágata has attained the highest, most fulfilled, awakened mind since there is not any highest, most fulfilled, awakened mind to be attained. Subhuti, the highest, most fulfilled, awakened mind that the Tathágata has attained is neither graspable nor elusive. This is why the Tathágata has said, 'All dharmas are Buddha dharma.' What are called all dharmas are, in fact, not all dharmas. That is why they are called all dharmas.

"Subhuti, a comparison can be made with the idea of a great human body."

Subhuti said, "What the Tathágata calls a great human body is, in fact, not a great human body."

"Subhuti, it is the same concerning bodhisattvas. If a bodhisattva thinks that she has to liberate all living beings, then she is not yet a bodhisattva. Why? Subhuti, there is no independently existing object of mind called bodhisattva. Therefore, the Buddha has said that all dharmas are without a self, a person, a living being, or a life span. Subhuti, if a bodhisattva thinks, 'I have to create a serene and beautiful Buddha field?, that person is not yet a bodhisattva. Why? What the Tathágata calls a serene and beautiful Buddha field is not in fact a serene and beautiful Buddha field. And that is why it is called a serene and beautiful Buddha field. Subhuti, any bodhisattva who thoroughly understands the principle of non-self and non-dharma is called by the Tathágata an authentic bodhisattva."

"Subhuti, what do you think? Does the Tathágata have the human eye?"

Subhuti replied, "Yes, World-Honored One, the Tathágata does have the human eye."

The Buddha asked, "Subhuti, what do you think? Does the Tathágata have the divine eye?"

Subhuti said, "Yes, World-Honored One, the Tathágata does have the divine eye."

"Subhuti, what do you think? Does the Tathágata have the eye of insight?"

Subhuti replied, "Yes, World-Honored One, the Tathágata does have the eye of insight."

"Subhuti, what do you think? Does the Tathágata have the eye of transcendent wisdom?"

"Yes, World-Honored One, the Tathágata does have the eye of transcendent wisdom."

The Buddha asked, "Does the Tathágata have the Buddha eye?"

"Yes, World-Honored One, the Tathágata does have the Buddha eye."

"Subhuti, what do you think? Does the Buddha see the sand in the Ganges as sand?"

Subhuti said, "World-Honored One, the Tathágata also calls it sand."

"Subhuti, if there were as many Ganges Rivers as the number of grains of sand of the Ganges and there was a Buddha land for each grain of sand in all those Ganges Rivers, would those Buddha lands be many?"

"Yes, World-Honored One, very many."

The Buddha said, "Subhuti, however many living beings there are in all these Buddha lands, though they each have a different mentality, the Tathágata understands them all. Why is that? Subhuti, what the Tathágata calls different mentalities are not in fact different mentalities. That is why they are called different mentalities."

"Why? Subhuti, the past mind cannot be grasped, neither can the present mind or the future mind."

"What do you think, Subhuti? If someone were to fill the 3,000 chiliocosms with precious treasures as an act of generosity, would that person bring great happiness by his virtuous act?" "Yes, very much, World-Honored One."

"Subhuti, if such happiness were conceived as an entity separate from everything else, the Tathágata would not have said it to be great, but because it is ungraspable, the Tathágata has said that the virtuous act of that person brought about great happiness."

"Subhuti, what do you think? Can the Tathágata be perceived by his perfectly formed body?"

"No, World-Honored One. What the Tathágata calls a perfectly formed body is not in fact a perfectly formed body. That is why it is called a perfectly formed body."

"What do you think, Subhuti? Can the Tathágata be perceived by his perfectly formed physiognomy?"

"No, World-Honored One. It is impossible to perceive the Tathágata by any perfectly formed physiognomy. Why? Because what the Tathágata calls perfectly formed physiognomy is not in fact perfectly formed physiognomy. That is why it is called perfectly formed physiognomy."

"Subhuti, do not say that the Tathágata conceives the idea 'I will give a teaching?. Do not think that way. Why? If anyone says that the Tathágata has something to teach, that person slanders the Buddha because he does not understand what I say. Subhuti, giving a Dharma talk in fact means that no talk is given. This is truly a Dharma talk."

Then, Insight-Life Subhuti said to the Buddha, "World-Honored One, in the future, will there be living beings who will feel complete confidence when they hear these words?"

The Buddha said, "Subhuti, those living beings are neither living beings nor non-living beings. Why is that? Subhuti, what the Tathágata calls non-living beings are truly living beings."

Subhuti asked the Buddha, "World-Honored One, is the highest, most fulfilled, awakened mind that the Buddha attained the unattainable?"

The Buddha said, "That is right, Subhuti. Regarding the highest, most fulfilled, awakened mind, I have not attained anything. That is why it is called the highest, most fulfilled, awakened mind."

"Furthermore, Subhuti, that mind is everywhere equally. Because it is neither high nor low, it is called the highest, most fulfilled, awakened mind. The fruit of the highest, most fulfilled, awakened mind is realized through the practice of all wholesome actions in the spirit of non-self, non-person, non-living being, and non-life span. Subhuti, what are called wholesome actions are in fact not wholesome actions. That is why they are called wholesome actions."

"Subhuti, if someone were to fill the 3,000 chiliocosms with piles of the seven precious treasures as high as Mount Sumeru as an act of generosity, the happiness resulting from this is much less than that of another person who knows how to accept, practice, and explain the Vajracchedika Prajna paramita Sutra to others. The happiness resulting from the virtue of a person who practices this sutra, even if it is only a gatha of four lines, cannot be described by using examples or mathematics."

"Subhuti, do not say that the Tathágata has the idea, 'I will bring living beings to the shore of liberation.' Do not think that way, Subhuti. Why? In truth there is not one single being for the Tathágata to bring to the other shore. If the Tathágata were to think there was, he would be caught in the idea of a self, a person, a living being, or a life span. Subhuti, what the Tathágata calls a self essentially has no self in the way that ordinary persons think there is a self. Subhuti, the Tathágata does not regard anyone as an ordinary person. That is why he can call them ordinary persons."

"What do you think, Subhuti? Can someone meditate on the Tathágata by means of the thirty-two marks?"

Subhuti said, "Yes, World-Honored One. We should use the thirty-two marks to meditate on the Tathágata."

The Buddha said, "If you say that you can use the thirty-two marks to see the Tathágata, then the Cakravartin is also a Tathágata?"

Subhuti said, "World-Honored One, I understand your teaching. One should not use the thirty-two marks to meditate on the Tathágata."

Then the World-Honored One spoke this verse:

"Someone who looks for me in form or seeks me in sound
is on a mistaken path and cannot see the Tathágata."

"Subhuti, if you think that the Tathágata realizes the highest, most fulfilled, awakened mind and does not need to have all the marks, you are wrong. Subhuti, do not think in that way. Do not think that when one gives rise to the highest, most fulfilled, awakened mind, one needs to see all objects of mind as nonexistent, cut off from life. Please do not think in that way. One who gives rise to the highest, most fulfilled, awakened mind does not contend that all objects of mind are nonexistent and cut off from life."

"Subhuti, if a bodhisattva were to fill the 3,000 chiliocosms with the seven precious treasures, as many as the number of sand grains in the Ganges as an act of generosity, the happiness brought about by his or her virtue is less than that brought about by someone who has understood and wholeheartedly accepted the truth that all dharmas are of selfless nature and is able to live and bear fully this truth. Why is that, Subhuti? Because a bodhisattva does not need to build up virtue and happiness."

Subhuti asked the Buddha, "What do you mean, World-Honored One, when you say that a bodhisattva does not need to build up virtue and happiness?"

"Subhuti, a bodhisattva gives rise to virtue but is not caught in the idea of virtue and happiness. That is why the Tathágata has said that a bodhisattva does not need to build up virtue and happiness."

"Subhuti, if someone says that the World-Honored One comes, goes, sits, and lies down, that person has not understood what I have said. Why? The meaning of Tathágata is 'does not come from anywhere and does not go anywhere?. That is why he is called a Tathágata.

"Subhuti, if a daughter or son of a good family were to grind the 3,000 chilio-cosms to particles of dust, do you think there would be many particles?"

Subhuti replied, "World-Honored One, there would be many indeed. Why? If particles of dust had a real self-existence, the Buddha would not have called them particles of dust. What the Buddha calls particles of dust are not, in essence, particles of dust. That is why they can be called particles of dust. World-Honored One, what the Tathágata calls the 3,000 chiliocosms are not chiliocosms. That is why they are called chiliocosms. Why? If chiliocosms are real, they are a compound of particles under the conditions of being assembled into an object. That which the Tathágata calls a compound is not essentially a compound. That is why it is called a compound."

"Subhuti, what is called a compound is just a conventional way of speaking. It has no real basis. Only ordinary people are caught up in conventional terms."

"Subhuti, if anyone says that the Buddha has spoken of a self view, a person view, a living-being view, or a life span view, has that person understood my meaning?"

"No, World-Honored One. Such a person has not understood the Tathágata. Why? What the Tathágata calls a self view, a person view, a living-being view, or a life span view are not in essence a self view, a person view, a living-being view, or a life span view. That is why they are called a self view, a person view, a living-being view, or a life span view."

"Subhuti, someone who gives rise to the highest, most fulfilled, awakened mind should know that this is true of all dharmas, should see that all dharmas are like this, should have confidence in the understanding of all dharmas without any conceptions about dharmas. Subhuti, what is called a conception of dharmas, the Tathágata has said, is not a conception of dharmas. That is why it is called a conception of dharmas."

"Subhuti, if someone were to offer an immeasurable quantity of the seven treasures to fill the worlds as infinite as space as an act of generosity, the happiness resulting from that virtuous act would not equal the happiness resulting from a son or daughter of a good family who gives rise to the awakened mind and reads, recites, accepts, and puts into practice this sutra, and explains it to others, even if only a gatha of four lines. In what spirit is this explanation given? Without being caught up in signs, just according to things as they are, without agitation. Why is this?

"All composed things are like a dream,
a phantom, a drop of dew, a flash of lightning.
That is how to meditate on them,
that is how to observe them."

After they heard the Lord Buddha deliver this sutra, the Venerable Subhuti, the Bhikshus and Bhiksunis, laymen and laywomen, and gods and asuras, filled with joy and confidence, undertook to put these teachings into practice.

The Vajracchedika Prajna paramita Sutra
http://www.buddhistinformation.com/diamondsutra.htm

5.22   Wonderful Voice Bodhisattva

Emitting rays of light from tufts of hair on his head and between his eyebrows, the Buddha illuminated countless worlds to the East, and also the one beyond them where the Buddha Wisdom King of the Pure Flower Constellation and the bodhisattva Wonderful Voice lived. This bodhisattva, who already had many great accomplishments, including attaining millions of different kinds of concentrations, when illumined by Shakyamuni Buddha expressed to the Buddha of his land his desire to go the saha-world to pay tribute to Shakyamuni Buddha and visit various bodhisattvas. The Buddha there warned him that even though the saha-world is not smooth or clean and its Buddha and bodhisattvas are short, he should not disparage or make little of that world or think that its Buddha and bodhisattvas are inferior.

Then, through the power of his meditation, Wonderful Voice made eighty-four thousand gold and silver lotus flowers and other valuables appear not far from where Shakyamuni Buddha was sitting on Sacred Eagle Peak. Seeing them, Manjushri asked Shakyamuni Buddha what they signified. When the Buddha explained that the flowers meant that Wonderful Voice Bodhisattva was coming to visit, Manjushri wanted to know what Wonderful Voice had done to gain such great powers and wanted to see him. And the Buddha said that Many Treasures Buddha would summon him.

Summoned by Many Treasures Buddha to come to see Manjushri, this extremely tall and handsome Wonderful Voice Bodhisattva, accompanied by eighty thousand other bodhisattvas, came to the saha-world on a flying platform of the seven valuable materials, passing though all the worlds to the East, where the grounds quaked in the six ways, flowers rained down from the heavens, drums sounded in the heavens, etc. Arriving at Sacred Eagle Peak, he descended from the platform, approached Shakyamuni Buddha, worshipped at his feet, presented him with a magnificent necklace, delivered various greetings and felicitations from the Buddha Wisdom King of the Pure Flower Constellation, and expressed the desire to see Many Treasures Buddha.

Many Treasures, in turn, praised him for coming. Then the bodhisattva Flower Virtue wanted to know what Wonderful Voice had done to merit such great powers.

Shakyamuni Buddha explained that once upon a time there was a Buddha named King of the Sound of Thunder in the Clouds in whose realm the Bodhisattva Wonderful Voice lived. Because he offered many kinds of beautiful music and jeweled bowls to the Buddha King of the Sound of Thunder in the Clouds, he was reborn in the land of the Buddha Wisdom King of the Pure Flower Constellation and was able to obtain great, divine powers. This bodhisattva is none other than the present bodhisattva Wonderful Voice. In previous lives he had taken many different forms— including women and girls, animals, gods and other heavenly beings, Buddhas, etc.— in order to teach the Lotus Sutra. He protects all living beings by taking whatever form— shravaka, pratyekabuddha, bodhisattva, Buddha—is appropriate for teaching them the Lotus Sutra.

When the Buddha taught this chapter, the eighty-four thousand who had come with Wonderful Voice and numerous other bodhisattvas of the saha-world won the ability to transform themselves into other living beings. Then Wonderful Voice made offerings to Shakyamuni Buddha and to the stupa of Many Treasures Buddha, and returned home to the land of Wisdom King of the Pure Flower Constellation Buddha and reported to him.

Summary of The Sutra of the Lotus Flower of The Wonderful Dharma. Dharma Wheel http://www.ibc-rk.org/chapter%2024.htm

5.23 Hymn to Perfect Wisdom

(Arya Bhagavati Prajnaparamita Hrdaya Sutram)

I - Homage to the Holy Perfection of Wisdom!

Thus have I heard. At one time
The Lord was staying at Rajagriha on
Vulture Peak Mountain
together with a great host of monks
and a great host of Bodhisattvas.
At that time, the Lord was composed in the concentration
on the course of Dharmas called Profound Illumination.

II - At that time also, the noble Lord Avalokiteshvara,
the Bodhisattva and Mahasattva,
in the practice of the profound Perfection of Wisdom
looked down; he beheld but five skandhas
and that in their own-being they were empty.
Then, through the inspiration of the Buddha,

the elder Sariputra said to the noble Lord Avalokiteshvara, the Bodhisattva and Mahasattva,

"How should any son of good family train who wishes

to engage in the practice of the profound Perfection of Wisdom?"

And the noble Lord Avalokiteshvara, the Bodhisattva and Mahasattva, spoke to the elder Sariputra as follows:

"Sariputra, any son or daughter of good family who wishes to engage in the practice of the profound Perfection of Wisdom should look upon it thus: he (or she) beholds but five skandhas and that in their own-being, they are empty.

III - "Form is emptiness, emptiness is form

Emptiness does not differ from form, and form does not differ from emptiness.

Likewise, feelings, recognition, volitions and consciousnesses are empty.

IV - "So, Sariputra, all dharmas are emptiness,

lacking differentiating marks; they are not produced nor stopped, not defiled and not immaculate, not deficient and not complete.

V - "Therefore, Sariputra, in emptiness there is no form,

no feeling, no recognition, no volition, no consciousness; no eye, no ear, no nose, no tongue, no body, no mind; no visible form, no sound, no smell no taste, no tangible, no mental object; no eye-element, etc., up to no mind-element, and no mental-consciousness element; no

ignorance and no extinction of ignorance, etc., up to no aging and death and no extinction of aging and death; likewise there is no Suffering, Origin, Cessation or Path, no wisdom-knowledge, no attainment and no non-attainment.

VI - "Therefore, Sariputra,

because there is no attainment, Bodhisattvas abide relying on the Perfection of Wisdom, without obscuration of thought, and so are unafraid.

Transcending perverted views, they attain the end, Nirvana.

VII - "All Buddhas existing in the three times,

relying on the Perfection of Wisdom, fully awaken to the highest, perfect Enlightenment.

VIII - "Therefore, one should know that the mantra of the

Prajnaparamita is the mantra of great knowledge, the highest mantra, the unequalled mantra, the mantra which allays all suffering, the Truth, since it has nothing wrong. The mantra of the Prajnaparamita is proclaimed:

tayata om gate gate paragate parasamgate bodhi soha

IX - "In this way, Sariputra, should a Bodhisattva and

Mahasattva train in the profound Perfection of Wisdom."

Then the Lord rose from that concentration

and commended the noble Lord Avalokiteshvara, the Bodhisattva and Mahasattva, saying "Well done, well done, oh son of good family! So it is, oh son of good family, so it is. Just as you have taught, should the profound Perfection of Wisdom be practiced and all the Tathagatas will rejoice."

When the Lord had uttered this, the elder Sariputra,

the noble Lord Avalokiteshvara, the Bodhisattva and Mahasattva, and all the people present, including the devas, human beings, asuras and gandharvas were delighted and applauded the Lord's speech.

http://www.fpmt-osel.org/
    meditate/hrtsutra.htm
Osel Shen Phen Ling Tibetan Buddhist Center

5.24 Buddhist Texts from China and Japan

One day the Patriarch sent for his disciples, Fa Hai, Zhi Cheng, Fa Da, Shen Hui, Zhi Chang, Zhi Tong, Zhi Che, Zhi Dao, Fa Zhen, Fa Ru, etc., and addressed them as follows:—

"You men are different from the common lot. After my entering into Parinirvana, each of you will be the Dhyana Master of a certain district. I am, therefore, going to give you some hints on preaching, so that when doing so, you may keep up the tradition of our School.

"First mention the three categories of Dharmas, and then the thirty-six 'pairs of opposites' in the activities (of the Essence of Mind). Then teach how to avoid the two extremes of 'coming in' or 'going out'. In all preaching, stray not from the Essence of Mind. Whenever a man puts a question to you, answer him in antonyms, so that a 'pair of opposites' will be formed. (For example), 'coming' and 'going' are the reciprocal cause of each other; when the interdependence of the two is entirely done away with there would be, in the absolute sense, neither 'coming' nor 'going'.

"The three categories of Dharmas are:—

Skandhas (aggregates),
Ayatanas (places or spheres of meeting),
Dhatus (factors of consciousness).

The five Skandhas are:—

Rupa (matter), Vedana (sensation), Samjna (perception), Samskara (tendencies of mind), and Vijnana (consciousness).

The twelve Ayatanas are:—

Six Sense Objects (external)	*Six Sense Organs (internal)*
Object of sight	Organ of sight
Object of hearing	Organ of hearing
Object of smell	Organ of smell
Object of taste	Organ of taste
Object of touch	Organ of touch
Object of thought	Organ of thought

The eighteen Dhatus are:

The six sense objects, six sense organs and six recipient vijnanas.

"Since the Essence of Mind is the embodiment of all Dharmas, it is called the Repository Consciousness (Alaya). But as soon as the process of thinking or reasoning is started, the Essence of Mind is transmuted into (various) vijnanas. When the six recipient vijnanas come into being, they perceive the six sense objects through the six 'doors' (of sense). Thus, the functioning of the eighteen dhatus derive their impetus from the Essence of Mind. Whether they function with an evil tendency or a good one depends upon what mood — good or evil — the Essence of Mind is in. Evil functioning is that of a common man, while good functioning is that of a Buddha. It is because there are 'pairs of opposites' inherent in the Essence of Mind that the functioning of the eighteen dhatus derive their impetus.

"The thirty-six 'Pairs of opposites' are:—

Five external inanimate ones: Heaven and earth, sun and moon, light and darkness, positive element and negative element, fire and water.

Twelve Dharmalaksana (phenomenal objects): Speech and Dharma, affirmation and negation, matter and non-matter, form and without form, taints (asravas) and absence of taint, matter and void, motion and quiescence, purity and impurity, ordinary people and sages, the Sangha and the laity, the aged and the young, the big and the small.

Nineteen pairs denoting the functioning of the Essence of Mind: Long and short, good and evil, infatuated and enlightened, ignorant and wise, perturbed and calm, merciful and wicked, abstinent (Sila) and indulgent, straight and crooked, full and empty, steep and level, Klesa and Bodhi, permanent and transient, compassionate and cruel, happy and angry, generous and mean, forward and backward, existent and non-existent, Dharmakaya and physical body, Sambhogakaya and Nirmanakaya.

"He who knows how to use these thirty-six pairs realizes the all-pervading principle which goes through the teaching of all Sutras. Whether he is 'coming in' or 'going out', he is able to avoid the two extremes.

"In the functioning of the Essence of Mind and in conversation with others, outwardly we should free ourselves from attachment to objects, whence come contact with objects; and inwardly, with regard to the teaching of the 'Void,' we should free ourselves from the idea of Nihilism. To believe in the reality of objects or in Nihilism would result in deep-rooted fallacious views or intensified ignorance respectively.

"A bigoted believer in Nihilism blasphemes against the Sutras on the ground that literature (*i.e.*, the Buddhist Scriptures) is unnecessary (for the study of Buddhism). If that were so, then neither would it be right for us to speak, since speech forms the substance of literature. He would also argue that in the direct method (literally, the straight Path) literature is discarded. But does he appreciate that the two words 'is discarded' are also literature? Upon hearing others speak of Sutras, such a man would criticize the speakers as 'addicted to scriptural authority'. It is bad enough for him to confine this mistaken notion to himself, but in addition, he blasphemes against the Buddhist scriptures. You men should know that it is a serious offence to speak ill of the Sutras, for the consequence is grave indeed!

"He who believes in the reality of outward objects tries to seek the form (from without) by practicing a certain system of doctrine. He may furnish spacious lecture-halls for the discussion of Realism or Nihilism, but such a man will not for numerous Kalpas realize the Essence of Mind.

"We should tread the Path according to the teaching of the Law, and not keep our mind in a state of indolence, thereby creating obstacles to the understanding of the Norm. To preach or to hear the Law without practicing it would give occasion for the arising of heretical views. Hence, we should tread the Path according to the teaching of the Law, and in the dissemination of the Dharma we should not be influenced by the concept of the reality of objects.

"If you understand what I say, and make use of it in preaching, in practice, and in your daily life, you will grasp the distinguishing feature of our School.

"Whenever a question is put to you, answer it in the negative if it is an affirmative one; and vice versa. If you are asked about an ordinary man, tell the enquirer something about a sage; and vice versa. From the correlation or interdependence of the two opposites the doctrine of the 'Mean' may be grasped. If all other questions are answered in this manner, you will not be far away from the truth.

"(Let me explain more fully). Suppose someone asks you what is darkness, answer him thus: Light is the Hetu (root condition) and darkness is the pratyaya (Conditions which bring about any given phenomenon). When light disappears, darkness is the consequence. The two are in contrast to each other. From the correlation or interdependence of the two the doctrine of the 'Mean' arises.

"In this way all other questions are to be answered. To ensure the perpetuation of the aim and object of our School in the transmission of the Dharma to your successors, this instruction should be handed down from one generation to another."

http://www.sinc.sunysb.edu/Clubs/buddhism/huineng/huineng10.html
From the Buddhist Association of the United States

Taoism and  *Confucianism*

6.1   Taoist Texts

6.11   On Tolerance

There has been such a thing as letting mankind alone and tolerance; there has never been such a thing as governing mankind. Letting alone Springs from the fear lest men's natural dispositions be perverted and tolerance springs from the fear lest their character be corrupted. But if their natural dispositions be not perverted, nor their character corrupted, what need is there left for government?

Of old, when Yao governed the empire, he made the people live happily; consequently the people struggled to be happy and became restless. When Chieh governed the empire he made the people live miserably; consequently the people regarded life as a burden and were discontented. Restlessness and discontent are subversive of virtue; and without virtue there has never been such a thing as stability.

When man rejoices greatly, he gravitates towards yang (the positive pole). When he is in great anger, he gravitates towards yin (the negative pole). If the equilibrium of positive and negative is disturbed, the four seasons are upset, and the balance of heat and cold is destroyed, man himself suffers physically thereby. It causes men to rejoice and sorrow inordinately, to live disorderly lives, to be vexed in their thoughts, and to lose their balance and form of conduct. When that happens, then the whole world seethes with revolt and discontent, and we have such men as Robber Cheh, Tseng, and Shih. Offer the entire world as rewards for the good or threaten the wicked with the dire punishments of the entire world, and it is still insufficient (to reform them). Consequently, with the entire world, one cannot furnish sufficient inducements or deterrents to action. From the Three Dynasties downwards, the world has lived in a helter-skelter of promotions and punishments. What chance have the people left for living the even tenor of their lives?

Besides, love (over-refinement) of vision leads to debauchery in color; love of hearing leads to debauchery in sound; love of charity leads to confusion in virtue; love of duty leads to perversion of principles; love of ceremonies (li) leads to a common fashion for technical skill; love of music leads to common lewdness of thought; love of wisdom leads to a fashion for the arts; and love of knowledge leads to a fashion for criticism If the people are allowed to live out the even tenor of their lives, the above eight may or may not be; it matters not. But if the people are not allowed to live out the even tenor of their lives, then these eight cause discontent and contention and strife, and throw the world into chaos.

Yet the world worships and cherishes them. Indeed deep-seated is the mental chaos of the world. Is it merely a passing mistake that can be simply removed? Yet they observe fasts before their discussion, bend down on their knees to practise them, and sing and beat the drum and dance to celebrate them. What can I do about it?

Therefore, when a gentleman is unavoidably compelled to take charge of the government of the empire, there is nothing better than inaction (letting alone). By means of inaction only can he allow the people to live out the even tenor of their lives. Therefore he who values the world as his own self may then be entrusted with the government of the world and he who loves the world as his own self may then be entrusted with the care of the world. {56} Therefore if the gentleman can refrain from disturbing the internal economy of man, and from glorifying the powers of sight and hearing, he can sit still like a corpse or spring into action like a dragon, be silent as the deep or talk with the voice of thunder, the movements of his spirit calling forth the natural mechanism of Heaven. He can remain calm and leisurely doing nothing, while all things are brought to maturity and thrive. What need then would have I to set about governing the world?

Ts'ui Chu: asked Lao Tan {57} , saying, "If the empire is not to be governed, how are men's hearts to be kept good?"

"Be careful," replied Lao Tan, "not to interfere with the natural goodness of the heart of man. Man's heart may be forced down or stirred up. In each case the issue is fatal. By gentleness, the hardest heart may be softened. But try to cut and polish it, and it will glow like fire or freeze like ice. In the twinkling of an eye it will pass beyond the limits of the Four Seas. In repose, it is profoundly still; in motion, it flies up to the sky. Like an unruly horse, it cannot be held in check. Such is the human heart."

Of old, the Yellow Emperor first interfered with the natural goodness of the heart of man, by means of charity and duty. In consequence, Yao and Shun wore the hair off their legs and the flesh off their arms in endeavoring to feed their people's bodies. They tortured the people's internal economy in order to conform to charity and duty. They exhausted the people's energies to live in accordance with the laws and statutes. Even then they did not succeed. Thereupon, Yao (had to) confine Huan-tou on Mount Ts'ung, exile the chiefs of the Three Miaos and their people into the Three Weis, and banish the Minister of Works to Yutu, which shows he had not succeeded. When it came to the times of the Three Kings, {58} the empire was in a state of foment. Among the bad men were Chieh and Cheh; among the good were Tseng and Shih. By and by, the Confucianists and the Motseanists arose; and then came confusion between joy and anger, fraud between the simple and the cunning, recrimination between the virtuous and the evil-minded, slander between the honest and the liars, and the world order collapsed. Then the great virtue lost its unity, men's lives were frustrated. When there was a general rush for knowledge, the people's desires ever went beyond their possessions. The next thing was then to invent axes and saws, to kill by laws and statutes, to disfigure by chisels and awls. The empire seethed with discontent, the blame for which rests upon those who would interfere with the natural goodness of the heart of man.

In consequence, virtuous men sought refuge in mountain caves, while rulers of great states sat trembling in their ancestral halls. Then, when dead men lay about pillowed on each other's corpses, when cangued prisoners jostled each other in crowds and condemned criminals were seen everywhere, then the Confucianists and the Motseanists bustled about and rolled up their sleeves in the midst of gyves and fetters! Alas, they know not shame, nor what it is to blush!

Until I can say that the wisdom of Sages is not a fastener of cangues, and that charity of heart and duty to one's neighbor are not bolts for gyves, how should I know that Tseng and Shih were not the singing arrows {59} (forerunners) of (the gangsters) Chieh and Cheh? Therefore it is said, "Abandon wisdom and discard knowledge, and the empire will be at peace."

The Yellow Emperor sat on the throne for nineteen years, and his laws obtained all over the empire. Hearing that Kuangch'engtse was living on Mount K'ungt'ung, he went there to see him, and said, "I am told that you are in possession of perfect Tao. May I ask what is the essence of this perfect Tao? I desire to obtain the essence of the universe to secure good harvests and feed my people. I should like also to control the yin and yang principles to fulfil the life of all living things."

"What you are asking about," replied Kuangch'engtse, "is merely the dregs of things. What you wish to control are the disintegrated factors thereof. Ever since the empire was governed by you, the clouds have rained before thickening, the foliage of trees has fallen before turning yellow, and the brightness of the sun and moon has increasingly paled. You have the shallowness of mind of a glib talker. How then are you fit to speak of perfect Tao?"

The Yellow Emperor withdrew. He resigned the Throne. He built himself a solitary hut, and sat upon white straw. For three months he remained in seclusion, and then went again to see Kuangch'engtse.

The latter was lying with his head towards the south. The Yellow Emperor approached from below upon his knees. Kowtowing twice upon the ground, he said, "I am told that you are in possession of perfect Tao. May I ask how to order one's life so that one may have long life?"

Kuangch'engtse jumped up with a start. "A good question indeed!" cried he. "Come, and I will speak to you of perfect Tao. The essence of perfect Tao is profoundly mysterious; its extent is lost in obscurity. "See nothing; hear nothing; guard your spirit in quietude and your body will go right of its own accord.

"Be quiet, be pure; toil not your body, perturb not your vital essence, and you will live for ever.

"For if the eye sees nothing, and the ear hears nothing, and the mind thinks nothing, your spirit will stay in your body, and the body will thereby live for ever.

"Cherish that which is within you, and shut off that which is without for much knowledge is a curse.

"Then I will take you to that abode of Great Light to reach the Plateau of Absolute Yang. I will lead you through the Door of the Dark Unknown to the Plateau of the Absolute Yin.

"The Heaven and Earth have their separate functions. The yin and yang have their hidden root. Guard carefully your body, and material things will prosper by themselves.

"I guard the original One, and rest in harmony with externals. Therefore I have been able to live for twelve hundred years and my body has not grown old."

The Yellow Emperor kowtowed twice and said, "Kuangch'engtse is surely God.

"Come," said Kuangch'engtse, "I will tell you. That thing is eternal; yet all men think it mortal. That thing is infinite; yet all men think it finite. Those who possess my Tao are princes in this life and rulers in the hereafter. Those who do not possess my Tao behold the light of day in this life and become clods of earth in the hereafter.

"Nowadays, all living things spring from the dust and to the dust return. But I will lead you through the portals of Eternity to wander in the great wilds of Infinity. My light is the light of sun and moon. My life is the life of Heaven and Earth. Before me all is nebulous; behind me all is dark, unknown. Men may all die, but I endure for ever."

When General Clouds was going eastwards, he passed through the branches of Fuyao (a magic tree) and happened to meet Great Nebulous. The latter was slapping his thighs and hopping about. When General Clouds saw him, he stopped like one lost and stood still, saying, "Who are you, old man, and what are you doing here?"

"Strolling!" replied Great Nebulous, still slapping his thighs and hopping about.

"I want to ask about something," said General Clouds.

"Ough!" uttered Great Nebulous.

"The spirits of Heaven are out of harmony," said General Clouds; "the spirits of the Earth are smothered; the six influences {61} of the weather do not work together, and the four seasons are no longer regular. I desire to blend the essence of the six influences and nourish all living beings. What am I to do?"

"I do not know! I do not know!" cried Great Nebulous, shaking his head, while still slapping his thighs and hopping about.

So General Clouds did not press his question. Three years later, when passing eastwards through the plains of the Sungs, he again fell in with Great Nebulous. The former was overjoyed, and hurrying up, said, "Has your Holiness {62} forgotten me? Has your Holiness forgotten me?" He then kowtowed twice and desired to be allowed to interrogate Great Nebulous; but the latter said, "I wander on without knowing what I want. I rush about without knowing whither I am going. I simply stroll about, watching unexpected events. What should I know?"

"I too regard myself as rushing about," answered General Clouds; "but the people follow my movements. I cannot escape the people and what I do they follow. I would gladly receive some advice."

"That the scheme of empire is in confusion," said Great Nebulous, "that the conditions of life are violated, that the will of the Dark Heaven is not accomplished, that the beasts of the field are scattered, that the birds of the air cry at night, that blight strikes the trees and herbs, that destruction spreads among the creeping things, — this, alas! is the fault of those who would rule others."

"True," replied General Clouds, "but what am I to do?"

"Ah!" cried Great Nebulous, "keep quiet and go home in peace!"

"It is not often," urged General Clouds, "that I meet with your Holiness. I would gladly receive some advice."

"Ah," said Great Nebulous, "nourish your heart. Rest in inaction, and the world will be reformed of itself. Forget your body and spit forth intelligence. Ignore all differences and become one with the Infinite. Release your mind, and free your spirit. Be vacuous, be devoid of soul. Thus will things grow and prosper and return to their Root. Returning to their Root without their knowing it, the result will be a formless whole which will never be cut up. To know it is to cut it up. Ask not about its name, inquire not into its nature, and all things will flourish of themselves."

"Your Holiness," said General Clouds, "has informed me with power and taught me silence. What I had long sought, I have now found." Thereupon he kowtowed twice and took leave.

The people of this world all rejoice in others being like themselves, and object to others being different from themselves. Those who make friends with their likes and do not make friends with their unlikes, are influenced by a desire to be above the others. But how can those who desire to be above the others ever be above the others? Rather than base one's Judgment on the opinions of the many, let each look after his own affairs. But those who desire to govern kingdoms clutch at the advantages of (the systems of) the Three Kings {63} without seeing the troubles involved. In fact, they are trusting the fortunes of a country to luck, but what country will be lucky enough to escape destruction? Their chances of preserving it do not amount to one in ten thousand, while their chances of destroying it are ten thousand to nothing and even more. Such, alas! is the ignorance of rulers.

For to have a territory is to have something great. He who has some thing great must not regard the material things as material things. Only by not regarding material things as material things can one be the lord of things. The principle of looking at material things as not real things is not confined to mere government of the empire. Such a one may wander at will between the six limits of space or travel over the Nine Continents unhampered and free. This is to be the Unique One. The Unique One is the highest among men.

The doctrine of the great man is (fluid) as shadow to form, as echo to sound. Ask and it responds, fulfilling its abilities as the help-mate of humanity. Noiseless in repose, objectless in motion, he brings you out of the confusion of your coming and going to wander in the Infinite. Formless in his movements, he is eternal with the sun. In respect of his bodily existence, he conforms to the universal standards. Through conformance to the universal standards, he forgets his own individuality. But if he forgets his individuality, how can he regard his possessions as possessions? Those who see possessions in possessions were the wise men of old. Those who regard not possessions as possessions are the friends of Heaven and Earth.

That which is low, but must be let alone, is matter. That which is humble, but still must be followed, is the people. That which is always there but still has to be attended to, is affairs. That which is inadequate, but still has to be set forth, is the law. That which is remote from Tao, but still claims our attention, is duty. That which is biassed, but must be broadened, is charity. Trivial, but requiring to be strengthened from within, that is ceremony. Contained within, but requiring to be uplifted, that is virtue. One, but not to be without modification, that is Tao. Spiritual, yet not to be devoid of action, that is God. Therefore the Sage looks up to God, but does not offer to aid. He perfects his virtue, but does not involve himself. He guides himself by Tao, but makes no plans. He identifies himself with charity, but does not rely on it. He performs his duties towards his neighbors, but does not set store by them. He responds to ceremony, without avoiding it. He undertakes affairs without declining them, and metes out law without confusion. He relies on the people and does not make light of them. He accommodates himself to matter and does not ignore it. Things are not worth attending to, yet they have to be attended to. He who does not understand God will not be pure in character. He who has not clear apprehension of Tao will not know where to begin. And he who is not enlightened by Tao, —alas indeed for him! What then is Tao? There is the Tao of God, and there is the Tao of man. Honour through inaction comes from the Tao of God: entanglement through action comes from the Tao of man. The Tao of God is fundamental: the Tao of man is accidental. The distance which separates them is great. Let us all take heed thereto!

From the Buddhist Association of the United States in
http://www.clas.ufl.edu/users/gthursby/taoism/cz-text2.htm#ON

6.12 Selections from the Tao-te Ching

25

Before the universe was born
there was something in the chaos of the heavens.
It stands alone and empty,
solitary and unchanging.
It is ever present and secure.
It may be regarded as the Mother of the universe.
Because I do not know its name,

I call it Dharma.
If forced to give it a name,
I would call it 'Great'.

Because it is Great means it is everywhere.
Being everywhere means it is eternal.
Being eternal means everything returns to it.

Dharma is great.
Heaven is great.
Earth is great.
Humanity is great.
Within the universe, these are the four great things.

Humanity follows the earth.
Earth follows Heaven.
Heaven follows the Dharma.
The Dharma follows only itself

30

Those who lead people by following the Dharma
don't use weapons to enforce their will.
Using force always leads to unseen troubles.

In the places where armies march,
thorns and briars bloom and grow.
After armies take to war,
bad years must always follow.
The skillful commander
strikes a decisive blow then stops.
When victory is won over the enemy
through war
it is not a thing of great pride.
When the battle is over,
arrogance is the new enemy.

War can result when no other alternative
is given,
so the one who overcomes an enemy
should not dominate them.
The strong always weakened with time.

This is not the way of the Dharma.
That which is not of the Dharma will
soon end.

34

The great Dharma flows unobstructed in
every direction.
All things rely on it to conceive and be
born,
and it does not deny even the smallest of
creation.
When it has accomplished great wonders,
it does not claim them for itself.
It nourishes infinite worlds,
yet it doesn't seek to master the smallest
creature.
Since it is without wants and desires,
it can be considered humble.
All of creation seeks it for refuge
yet it does not seek to master or control.
Because it does not seek greatness;
it is able to accomplish truly great
things.

Tao Te Ching - Written by Lao-Tzu
The Way of Dharma and It's Power
A New Translation
For the Public Domain
by J. H. McDonald

http://www.geocities.com/shoshindojo/

6.2   Confucian Texts

6.21   Selections from the Analects of Confucius

Master K'ung said of the head of the Chi family when he had eight teams of dancers performing in his courtyard, "If this man can be endured, who cannot be endured!"

The Three Families used the Yung Song during the removal of the sacrificial vessels. The master said,

"By rulers and lords attended,
The Son of Heaven, mysterious——"

What possible application can such words have in the hall of the Three Families?

The Master said, "A man who is not Good, what can he have to do with ritual? A man who is not Good, what can he have to do with music?"

Lin Fang asked for some main principles in connection with ritual. The Master said, "A very big question. In ritual at large it is a safe rule always to be too sparing rather than too lavish; and in the particular case of mourning-rites, they should be dictated by grief rather than fear."

The Master said, "The barbarians of the East and North have retained their princes. They are not in such a state of decay as we in China."

The head of the Chi family was going to make the offerings on Mount T'ai. The Master said to Jan Ch'iu, "Cannot you save him from this?" Jan Ch'iu replied, "I cannot." The Master said, "Alas, we can hardly suppose Mount T'ai to be ignorant of matters that even Lin Fang inquires into!"

The Master said, "Gentlemen never compete. You will say that in archery they do so. But even then they bow and make way for one another when they are going up to the archery-ground, when they are coming down and at the subsequent drinking-bout. Thus even when competing, they still remain gentlemen."

Tzu-hsia asked saying, "What is the meaning of

Oh the sweet smile dimpling,
The lovely eyes so black and white!
Plain silk that you would take for colored stuff."

The Master said, "The painting comes after the plain groundwork." Tzu-hsia said, "Then ritual comes afterwards?" The Master said, "Shang it is who bears me up. At last I have someone with whom I can discuss the Songs!"

Someone asked for an explanation of the Ancestral Sacrifice. The Master said, "I do not know. Anyone who knew the explanation could deal with all things under Heaven as easily as I lay this here"; and he laid his finger upon the palm of his hand.

Of the saying, "The word 'sacrifice' is like the word 'present': one should sacrifice to a spirit as though that spirit was present," the Master said, "If I am not present at the sacrifice, it is as though there were no sacrifice."

Wang-sun Chia asked about the meaning of the saying,

"Better pay court to the stove
Than pay court to the Shrine."

The Master said, "It is not true. He who has put himself in the wrong with Heaven has no means of expiation left."

The Master said, "Chou could survey the two preceding dynasties. How great a wealth of culture! And we follow upon Chou."

When the Master entered the Grand Temple he asked questions about everything there. Someone said, "Do not tell me that this son of a villager from Tsou is expert in matters of ritual. When he went to the Grand Temple, he had to ask about everything." The Master hearing of this said, "Just so! such is the ritual." The Master said, "The saying

In archery it is not the hide that counts,
For some men have more strength than others,
is the way of the Ancients."

Tzu-kung wanted to do away with the presentation of a sacrificial sheep at the announcement of each new moon. The Master said, "Ssu! You grudge sheep, but I grudge ritual."

The Master said, "Were anyone to-day to serve his prince according to the full prescriptions of ritual, he would be thought a sycophant."

When talking to the Grand Master of Lu about music, the Master said, "Their music in so far as one can find out about it began with a strict unison. Soon the musicians were given more liberty; but the tone remained harmonious, brilliant, consistent, right on till the close."

The Master spoke of the Succession Dance as being perfect beauty and at the same time perfect goodness; but of the War Dance as being perfect beauty, but not perfect goodness.

The Master said, "High office filled by men of narrow views, ritual performed without reverence, the forms of mourning observed without griefthese things I cannot bear to see!"

The Master said, "It is Goodness that gives to a neighborhood its beauty. One who is free to choose, yet does not prefer to dwell among the Good-how can he be accorded the name of wise?"

The Master said, "Without Goodness a man

Cannot for long endure adversity,
Cannot for long enjoy prosperity."

The Good Man rests content with Goodness; he that is merely wise pursues Goodness in the belief that it pays to do so.

Of the adage "Only a Good Man knows how to like people, knows how to dislike them," the Master said, "He whose heart is in the smallest degree set upon Goodness will dislike no one."

"Wealth and rank are what every man desires, but if they can only be retained to the detriment of the Way he professes, he must relinquish them. Poverty and obscurity are what every man detests, but if they can only be avoided to the detriment of the Way he professes, he must accept them. The gentleman who ever parts company with Goodness does not fulfill that name. Never for a moment does a gentleman quit the way of Goodness. He is never so harried but that he cleaves to this, never so tottering but that he cleaves to this."

The Master said, "I for my part have never yet seen one who really cared for Goodness, nor one who really abhorred wickedness. One who really cared for Goodness would never let any other consideration come first. One who abhorred wickedness would be so constantly doing Good that wickedness would never have a chance to get at him. Has anyone ever managed to do Good with his whole might even as long as the space of a single day? I think not. Yet I for my part have never seen anyone give up such an attempt because he had not the strength to go on. It may well have happened, but I for my part have never seen it."

The Master said, "Every man's faults belong to a set. If one looks out for faults, it is only as a means of recognizing Goodness."

The Master said, "In the morning, hear the Way; in the evening, die content!"

The Master said, "A Knight whose heart is set upon the Way, but who is ashamed of wearing shabby clothes and eating coarse food, is not worth calling into counsel."

The Master said, "A gentleman in his dealings with the world has neither enmities nor affections; but wherever he sees Right he ranges himself beside it."

The Master said, "Where gentlemen set their hearts upon moral force (tê), the commoners set theirs upon the soil. Where gentlemen think only of punishments, the commoners think only of exemptions."

The Master said, "Those whose measure are dictated by mere expediency will arouse continual discontent."

The Master said, "If it is really possible to govern countries by ritual and yielding, there is no more to be said. But if it is not really possible, of what use is ritual?"

The Master said, "He does not mind not being in office; all he minds about is whether he has qualities that entitle him to office. He does not mind failing to get recognition; he is too busy doing the things that entitle him to recognition."

The Master said, "Shên! My Way has one (thread) that runs right through it." Master Tsêng said, "Yes." When the Master had gone out, the disciples asked, saying "What did he mean?" Master Tsêng said, "Our Master's Way is simply this: Loyalty, consideration."

The Master said, "A gentleman takes as much trouble to discover what is right as lesser men take to discover what will pay."

The Master said, "In the presence of a good man, think all the time how you may learn to equal him. In the presence of a bad man, turn your gaze within! The

Master said, "In serving his father and mother a man may gently remonstrate with them. But if he sees that he has failed to change their opinion, he should resume an attitude of deference and not thwart them; may feel discouraged, but not resentful."

The Master said, "While father and mother are alive, a good son does not wander far afield; or if he does so, goes only where he has said he was going." The Master said, "If for the whole three years of mourning a son manages to carry on the household exactly as in his father's day, then he is a good son indeed."

The Master said, "It is always better for a man to know the age of his parents. In the one case such knowledge will be a comfort to him; in the other, it will fill him with a salutary dread."

The Master said, "In old days a man kept a hold on his words, fearing the disgrace that would ensue should he himself fail to keep pace with them."

The Master said, "Those who err on the side of strictness are few indeed!"

The Master said, "A gentleman covets the reputation of being slow in word but prompt in deed."

The Master said, "Moral force *(tê)* never dwells in solitude; it will always bring neighbors."

Yzu-yu said, "In the service of one's prince repeated scolding can only lead to loss of favor; in friendship, it can only lead to estrangement."

6.22   The Meaning and Value of Rituals

One of the greatest interpreters of Confucius was Hsün tzû. In the following section, Hsün tzû states the Confucian view of the value rituals have for a society.

Rites (li) rest on three bases: Heaven and earth, which are the source of all life; the ancestors, who are the source of the human race; sovereigns and teachers, who are the source of government. If there were no Heaven and earth, where would life come from? If there were no ancestors, where would the offspring come from? If there were no sovereigns and teachers, where would government come from? Should any of the three be missing, either there would be no men or men would be without peace. Hence rites are to serve Heaven on high and earth below, and to honour the ancestors and elevate the sovereigns and teachers. Herein lies the threefold basis for rites.

In general rites begin with primitive practices, attain cultured forms, and finally achieve beauty and felicity. When rites are at their best, men's emotions and sense of beauty are both fully expressed. When they are at the next level, either the emotion or the sense of beauty oversteps the others. When they are at still the next level, emotion reverts to the state of primitivity.

It is through rites that Heaven and earth are harmonious and sun and moon are bright, that the four seasons are ordered and the stars are on their courses, that rivers flow and that things prosper, that love and hatred are tempered and joy and anger are in keeping. They cause the lowly to be obedient and those on high to be illustrious. He who holds to the rites is never confused in the midst of multifarious change; he who deviates therefrom is lost. Rites-are they not the culmination of culture?

Rites require us to treat both life and death with attentiveness. Life is the beginning of man, death is his end. When a man is well off both at the end and the beginning, the way of man is fulfilled. Hence the gentleman respects the beginning and is carefully attentive to the end. To pay equal attention to the end as well as to the beginning is the way of the gentleman and the beauty of rites and righteousness.

Rites serve to shorten that which is too long and lengthen that which is too short, reduce that which is too much and augment that which is too little, express the beauty of love and reverence and cultivate the elegance of righteous conduct. Therefore, beautiful adornment and coarse sackcloth, music and weeping, rejoicing and sorrow, though pairs of opposites, are in the rites equally utilized and alternately brought into play. Beautiful adornment, music, and rejoicing are appropriate on occasions of felicity; coarse sackcloth, weeping, and sorrow are appropriate on occasions of ill-fortune. Rites make room for beautiful adornment but not to the point of being fascinating, for coarse sackcloth but not to the point of deprivation or self-injury, for music and rejoicing but not to the point of being lewd and indolent, for weeping and sorrow but not to the point of being depressing and injurious. Such is the middle path of rites.

Funeral rites are those by which the living adorn the dead. The dead are accorded a send-off as though they were living. In this way the dead are served like the living, the absent like the present. Equal attention is thus paid to the end as well as to the beginning of life.

Now the rites used on the occasion of birth are to embellish joy, those used on the occasion of death are to embellish sorrow, those used at sacrifice are to embellish reverence, those used on military occasions are to embellish dignity.

Shinto

7.1   The Kojiki

[B.H. Chamberlain, translator 1882]

PART I.- THE BIRTH OF THE DEITIES

THE BEGINNING OF HEAVEN AND EARTH

The names of the deities that were born in the Plain of High Heaven when the Heaven and Earth began were the deity Master-of-the-August-Center-of-Heaven; next, the High-August-Producing-Wondrous deity; next, the Divine-Producing-Won-drous deity. These three deities were all deities born alone, and hid their persons. The names of the deities that were born next from a thing that sprouted up like unto a reed-shoot when the earth, young and like unto floating oil, drifted about medusa-like, were the Pleasant-Reed-Shoot-Prince-Elder deity, next the Heavenly-Eternally-Standing deity. These two deities were likewise born alone, and hid their persons.

The five deities in the above list are separate Heavenly deities.

THE SEVEN DIVINE GENERATIONS

The names of the deities that were born next were the Earthly-Eternally-Stand-ing deity; next, the Luxuriant-Integrating-Master deity. These two deities were like-wise deities born alone, and hid their persons. The names of the deities that were born next were the deity Mud-Earth-Lord; next, his Younger sister the deity -Mud-Earth-Lady; next, the Germ-Integrating deity; next, his younger sister the Life-Inte-grating-Deity; next, the deity of Elder-of-the-Great-Place; next, his younger sister the deity Elder-Lady-of-the-Great-Place; next, the deity Perfect-Exterior; next, his younger sister the deity Oh-Awful-Lady; next, the deity Izanagi or the Male-Who-Invites; next, his younger sister Izanami or the deity the Female-Who-Invites.

From the Earthly-Eternally-Standing deity down to the deity the Female-Who-Invites in the previous list are what are termed the Seven Divine Generations.

THE ISLAND OF ONOGORO

Hereupon all the Heavenly deities commanded the two deities His Augustness the Male-Who-Invites and Her Augustness the Female-Who-Invites, ordering them to "make, consolidate, and give birth to this drifting land." Granting to them a heavenly jeweled spear, they thus deigned to charge them. So the two deities, standing upon the Floating Bridge of Heaven pushed down the jeweled spear and stirred with it, whereupon, when they had stirred the brine till it went curdle-curdle, and drew the spear up, the brine that dripped down from the end of the spear was piled up and became an island. This is the Island of Onogoro.

COURTSHIP OF THE DEITIES   THE MALE-WHO-INVITES AND THE FEMALE-WHO-INVITES

Having descended from Heaven on to this island, they saw to the erection of a heavenly august pillar, they saw to the erection of a hall of eight fathoms. Then Izanagi, the Male-Who-Invites, said to Izanami, the Female-Who-Invites, "We should create children"; and he said, "Let us go around the heavenly august pillar, and when we meet on the other side let us be united. Do you go around from the left, and I will go from the right." When they met, Her Augustness, the Female-Who-Invites, spake first, exclaiming, "Ah, what a fair and lovable youth!" Then His Augustness said, "Ah what a fair and lovable maiden!" But afterward he said, " It was not well that the woman should speak first!" The child which was born to them was Hiruko (the leech-child), which when three years old was still unable to stand upright. So they placed the leech-child in a boat of reeds and let it float away. Next they gave birth to the island of Aha. This likewise is not reckoned among their children.

Hereupon the two deities took counsel, saving: "The children to whom we have now given birth are not good. It will be best to announce this in the august place of the Heavenly deities." They ascended forthwith to Heaven and inquired of Their Augustnesses the Heavenly deities. Then the Heavenly deities commanded and found out by grand divination, and ordered them, saying: "they were not good because the woman spoke first. Descend back again and amend your words." So thereupon descending back, they again went round the heavenly august pillar. Thereupon his Augustness the Male-who-Invites spoke first: " Ah! what a fair and lovely maiden!" Afterward his younger sister Her Augustness the Female-Who-Invites spoke: " Ah! what a fair and lovely youth! " Next they gave birth to the Island of Futa-na in Iyo. This island has one body and four faces, and each face has a name. So the Land of Iyo is called Lovely-Princess; the Land of Sanuki is called Princess-Good-Boiled-Rice; the Land of Aha is called the Princess-of-Great-Food, the Land of Tosa is called Brave-Good-Youth. Next they gave birth to the islands of Mitsu-go near Oki, another name for which islands is Heavenly-Great-Heart-Youth. This island likewise has one body and four faces, and each face has a name. So the Land of Tsukushi is called White-Sun-Youth; the Land of Toyo is called Luxuriant-Sun-Youth; the Land of Hi is called Brave-Sun-Confronting-Luxuriant-Wondrous-Lord-Youth; the Land of Kumaso is called Brave-Sun-Youth. Next they gave birth to the Island of Iki, another name for which is Heaven's One-Pillar. Next they gave birth to the Island of Tsu, another name for which is Heavenly-Hand-Net-Good-Princess. Next they gave birth to the Island of Sado. Next they gave birth to Great-Yamato-the-Luxuriant-Island-of-the-Dragon-fly, another name for which is Heavenly-August-Sky-Luxuriant-Dragon-fly-Lord-Youth. The name of "Land-of-the-Eight-Great-Islands" therefore originated in these eight islands having been born first. After that, when they had returned, they gave birth to the Island of Koo-zhima in Kibi, another name for which island is Brave-Sun-Direction-Youth. Next they gave birth to the Island of Adzuki, another name for which is Oho-Nu-De-Hime. Next they gave birth to the Island of Oho-shima, another name for which is Oho-Tamaru-Wake. -Next they gave birth to the Island of Hime, another name for which is Heaven's-One-Root. Next they gave birth to the Island of Chika, another name for which is Heavenly-Great-Male. Next they gave birth to the islands of Futa-go, another name for which is Heaven's Two-Houses. (Six islands in all from the Island of Ko in Kibi to the Island of Heaven's-Two-Houses.)

BIRTH OF THE VARIOUS DEITIES

When they had finished giving birth to countries, they began afresh giving birth to deities. So the name of the deity they gave birth to was the deity Great-Male-of-the-Great-Thing; next, they gave birth to the deity Rock-Earth-Prince; next, they gave birth to the deity Rock-Nest-Princess; next, they gave birth to the deity Great-Door-Sun-Youth; next, they gave birth to the deity Heavenly-Blowing-Male; next, they gave birth to the deity Great-House-Prince; next, they gave birth to the deity Youth-of-the-Wind-Breath-the-Great-Male; next, they gave birth to the sea-deity, whose name is the deity Great-Ocean-Possessor next, they gave birth to the deity of the Water-Gates, whose name is the deity Prince-of-Swift-Autumn ; next they gave birth to his younger sister the deity Princess-of-Swift-Autumn. (Ten deities in all from the deity Great-Male-of-the-Great-Thing to the deity Princess-of-Autumn.) The names of the deities given birth to by these two deities Prince-of-Swift-Autumn and Princess-of-Swift-Autumn from their separate dominions of river and sea were: the deity Foam-Calm; next, the deity Foam-Waves; next the deity Bubble-Calm; next, the deity Bubble-Waves; next the deity Heavenly-Water-Divider; next, the deity Earthly-Water-Divider; next, the deity Heavenly-Water-Drawing-Gourd-Possessor; next, the deity Earthly-Water-Drawing-Gourd-Possessor. (Eight deities in all from the deity Foam-Prince to the deity Earthly-Water-Drawing-Gourd-Possessor.) Next, they gave birth to the deity of Wind, whose name is the deity Prince-of-Long-Wind. Next, they gave birth to the deity of Trees, whose name is deity Stem-Elder; next, they gave birth to the deity of Mountains, whose name is the deity Great-Mountain-Possessor. Next, they gave birth to the deity of Moors, whose name is the deity Thatch-Moor-Princess, another name for whom is the deity Moor-Elder. (Four deities in all from the deity Prince-of-long-wind to Moor-Elder.) The names of the deities given birth to by these two deities, the deity Great-Mountain-Possessor and the deity, Moor-Elder from their separate dominions of mountain and moor were: the deity Heavenly-Elder-of-the Passes; next, the deity Earthly-Elder-of-the-Passes; next, the deity Heavenly-Pass-Boundary; next, the deity Earthly-Pass-Boundary; next, the deity Heavenly-Dark-Door; next, the deity Earthly-Dark-Door next, the deity Great-Vale-Prince; next, the deity Great-Vale-Princess. (Eight deities in all from the deity Heavenly-Elder-of-the-Passes to the deity Great-Vale-Princess.) The name of the deity they next gave birth to was the deity Bird's-Rock-Camphor-tree-Boat, another name for whom is the Heavenly-Bird-Boat. Next, they gave birth to the deity Princess-of-Great-Food. Next, they gave birth to the Fire-Burning-Swift-Male deity, another name for whom is the deity Fire-Shining-Prince, and another name is the deity Fire-Shining-Elder.

RETIREMENT OF HER AUGUSTNESS THE PRINCESS-WHO-INVITES

Through giving birth to this child her august private parts were burned, and she sickened and lay down. The names of the deities born from her vomit were the deity Metal-Mountain-Prince and, next, the deity Metal-Mountain-Princess. The names of the deities that were born from her feces were the deity Clay-Viscid-Prince and, next, the deity Clay-Viscid-Princess. The names of the deities that were next born from her urine were the deity Mitsubanome and, next, the Young-Wondrous-Producing deity. The child of this deity was called the deity Luxuriant-Food-Princess. So the deity the Female-Who-Invites, through giving birth to the deity of Fire, at length divinely retired. (Eight deities in all from the Heavenly-Bird-Boat to the deity Luxuriant-Food-Princess.) The total number of islands given birth to jointly by the two deities the Male- Who-Invites and the Female-Who-Invites was fourteen, and of deities thirty-five. (These are such as were given birth to before the deity the Princess-Who-Invites divinely retired. Only the Island of Onogoro was not given birth to and, moreover, the Leech-Child and the Island of Aha are not reckoned among the children.)

So then His Augustness the Male-Who-Invites said: " Oh! Thine Augustness my lovely younger sister' Oh! that I should have exchanged thee for this single child! " And as he crept round her august pillow, and as he crept round her august feet and wept, there was born from his august tears the deity that dwells at Konomoto, near Unewo on Mount Kagu, and whose name is the Crying-Weeping-Female deity. So he buried the divinely retired deity the Female-Who-Invites on Mount Hiba, at the boundary of the Land of Idzumo and the Land of Hahaki.

TIIE SLAYING OF TIIE FIRE-DEITY

Then His Augustness the Male-Who-Invites, drawing the ten-grasp saber that was augustly girded on him, cut off the head of his child the deity Shining-Elder. Hereupon the names of the deities that were born from the blood that stuck to the point of the august sword and bespattered the multitudinous rock-masses were: the deity Rock-Splitter; next, the deity Root-Splitter; next, the Rock-Possessing-Male deity. The names of the deities that were next born from the blood that stuck to the upper part of the august sword and again bespattered the multitudinous rock-masses were: the Awfully-Swift deity; next, the Fire-Swift deity; next, the Brave-Awful-Possessing-Male deity, another name for whom is the Brave-Snapping deity, and another name is the Luxuriant-Snapping deity. The names of the deities that were next born from the blood that collected on the hilt of the august sword and leaked out between his fingers were: the deity Kura-okami and, next, the deity Kura-mitsuba.

All the eight deities in the above list, from the deity Rock-Splitter to the deity Kura-mitsuha, are deities that were born from the august sword.

The name of the deity that was born from the bead of the deity Shining-Elder, who bad been slain, was the deity Possessor-of-the-True-Pass-Mountains. The name of the deity that was next born from his chest was the deity Possessor-of-Descent—Mountains. The name of the deity that was next born from his belly was the deity Possessor-of-the-Innermost Mountains. The name of the deity that was next born from his private parts was the deity Possessor-of-the-Dark-Mountains. The name of the deity that was next born from his left hand was the deity Possessor-of-the-Densely-Wooded-Mountains. The name of the deity that was next born from his right hand was the deity Possessor-of-the-Outlying-Mountains. The name of the deity that was next born from his left foot was the deity Possessor-of-the-Moorland-Mountains. The name of the deity that was next born from his right foot was the deity Possessor-of-the-Outer—Mountains. (Eight deities in an from the deity Possessor-of-the-True-Pass-Mountains to the deity Possessor-of-the-Outer—Mountains.) So the name of the sword with which the -Male-Who-Invites cut off his son's head was Heavenly-Point-Blade-Extended, and another name was Majestic-Point-Blade-Extended.

http://www.sacred-texts.com/shi/kojiki.htm

Judaism

8.1 Selections from the Hebrew Bible

8.11 A Biblical Origin Tale

In the beginning when God created the heavens and the earth, the earth was a formless void and darkness covered the face of the deep, while a wind from God swept over the face of the waters. Then God said, "Let there be light"; and there was light. And God saw that the light was good; and God separated the light from the darkness. God called the light Day, and the darkness he called Night. And there was evening and there was morning, the first day.

And God said, "Let there be a dome in the midst of the waters, and let it separate the waters from the waters." So God made the dome and separated the waters that were under the dome from the waters that were above the dome. And it was so. God called the dome Sky. And there was evening and there was morning, the second day.

And God said, "Let the waters under the sky be gathered together into one place, and let the dry land appear." And it was so. God called the dry land Earth, and the waters that were gathered together he called Seas. And God saw that it was good. Then God said, "Let the earth put forth vegetation: plants yielding seed, and fruit trees of every kind on earth that bear fruit with the seed in it." And it was so. The earth brought forth vegetation: plants yielding seed of every kind, and trees of every kind bearing fruit with the seed in it. And God saw that it was good. And there was evening and there was morning, the third day.

And God said, "Let there be lights in the dome of the sky to separate the day from the night; and let them be for signs and for seasons and for days and years, and let them be lights in the dome of the sky to give light upon the earth." And it was so. God made the two great lights-the greater light to rule the day and the lesser light to rule the night-and the stars. God set them in the dome of the sky to give light upon the earth, to rule over the day and over the night, and to separate the light from the darkness. And God saw that it was good. And there was evening and there was morning, the fourth day.

And God said, "Let the waters bring forth swarms of living creatures, and let birds fly above the earth across the dome of the sky." So God created the great sea monsters and every living creature that moves, of every kind, with which the waters swarm, and every winged bird of every kind. And God saw that it was good. God blessed them, saying, "Be fruitful and multiply and fill the waters in the seas, and let birds multiply on the earth." And there was evening and there was morning, the fifth day.

And God said, "Let the earth bring forth living creatures of every kind: cattle and creeping things and wild animals of the earth of every kind." And it was so. God made the wild animals of the earth of every kind, and the cattle of every kind, and everything that creeps upon the ground of every kind. And God saw that it was good.

Then God said, "Let us make humankind in our image, according to our likeness; and let them have dominion over the fish of the sea, and over the birds of the air, and over the cattle, and over all the wild animals of the earth, and over every creeping thing that creeps upon the earth."

So God created humankind in his image, in the image of God he created them; male and female he created them.

God blessed them, and God said to them, "Be fruitful and multiply, and fill the earth and subdue it; and have dominion over the fish of the sea and over the birds of the air and over every living thing that moves upon the earth." God said, "See, I have given you every plant yielding seed that is upon the face of all the earth, and every tree with seed in its fruit; you shall have them for food.

And to every beast of the earth, and to every bird of the air, and to everything that creeps on the earth, everything that has the breath of life, I have given every green plant for food." And it was so.

God saw everything that he had made, and indeed, it was very good. And there was evening and there was morning, the sixth day.

Thus the heavens and the earth were finished, and all their multitude. And on the seventh day God finished the work that he had done, and he rested on the seventh day from all the work that he had done. So God blessed the seventh day and hallowed it, because on it God rested from all the work that he had done in creation.

These are the generations of the heavens and the earth when they were created.

8.12   Abraham: the Father of Many Nations

When Abram was ninety-nine years old, the LORD appeared to Abram, and said to him, "I am God Almighty; walk before me, and be blameless: And I will make my covenant between me and you, and will make you exceedingly numerous." Then Abram fell on his face; and God said to him,

"As for me, this is my covenant with you: You shall be the ancestor of a multitude of nations. No longer shall your name be Abram, but your name shall be Abraham; for I have made you the ancestor of a multitude of nations. I will make you exceedingly fruitful; and I will make nations of you, and kings shall come from you. I will establish my covenant between me and you, and your offspring after you throughout their generations, for an everlasting covenant, to be God to you and to your offspring after you. And I will give to you, and to your offspring after you, the land where you are now an alien, all the land of Canaan, for a perpetual holding; and I will be their God."

8.13   Exodus, the Scriptural Warrant for Passover

The LORD said to Moses and Aaron in the land of Egypt: This month shall mark for you the beginning of months; it shall be the first month of the year for you. Tell the whole congregation of Israel that on the tenth of this month they are to take a lamb for each family, a lamb for each household. If a household is too small for a whole lamb, it shall join its closest neighbor in obtaining one; the lamb shall be divided in proportion to the number of people who eat of it. Your lamb shall be without blemish, a year-old male; you may take it from the sheep or from the goats. You shall keep it until the fourteenth day of this month; then the whole assembled congregation of Israel shall slaughter it at twilight. They shall take some of the blood and put it on the two doorposts and the lintel of the houses in which they eat it. They shall eat the lamb that same night; they shall eat it roasted over the fire with unleavened bread and bitter herbs. Do not eat any of it raw or boiled in water, but roasted over the fire, with its head, legs, and inner organs. You shall let none of it remain until the morning; anything that remains until the morning you shall burn. This is how you shall eat it: your loins girded, your sandals on your feet, and your staff in your hand; and you shall eat it hurriedly. It is the passover of the LORD. For I will pass through the land of Egypt that night, and I will strike down every firstborn in the land of Egypt, both human beings and animals; on all the gods of Egypt I will execute judgments: I am the LORD. The blood shall be a sign for you on the houses where you live: when I see the blood, I will pass over you, and no plague shall destroy you when I strike the land of Egypt.

This day shall be a day of remembrance for you. You shall celebrate it as a festival to the LORD; throughout your generations you shall observe it as a perpetual ordinance. Seven days you shall eat unleavened bread; on the first day you shall remove leaven from your houses, for whoever eats leavened bread from the first day until the seventh day shall be cut off from Israel. On the first day you shall hold a solemn assembly, and on the seventh day a solemn assembly; no work shall be done on those days; only what everyone must eat, that alone may be prepared by you. You shall observe the festival of unleavened bread, for on this very day I brought your companies out of the land of Egypt: you shall observe this day throughout your generations as a perpetual ordinance. In the first month, from the evening of the fourteenth day until the evening of the twenty-first day, you shall eat unleavened bread. For seven days no leaven shall be found in your houses; for whoever eats what is leavened shall be cut off from the congregation of Israel, whether an alien or a native of the land. You shall eat nothing leavened; in all your settlements you shall eat unleavened bread.

Then Moses called all the elders of Israel and said to them, "Go, select lambs for your families, and slaughter the passover lamb. Take a bunch of hyssop, dip it in the blood that is in the basin, and touch the lintel and the two doorposts with the blood in the basin. None of you shall go outside the door of your house until morning. For the LORD will pass through to strike down the Egyptians; when he sees the blood on the lintel and on the two doorposts, the LORD will pass over that door and will not allow the destroyer to enter your houses to strike you down. You shall observe this rite as a perpetual ordinance for you and your children. When you come to the land that the LORD will give you, as he has promised, you shall keep this observance. And when your children ask you, 'What do you mean by this observance?' you shall say, 'It is the passover sacrifice to the LORD, for he passed over the houses of the Israelites in Egypt, when he struck down the Egyptians but spared our houses.'" And the people bowed down and worshiped.

The Israelites went and did just as the LORD had commanded Moses and Aaron.

8.14   Law and Ethics

And Moses summoned all Israel, and said to them, "Hear, O Israel, the statutes and the ordinances which I speak in your hearing this day, and you shall learn them and be careful to do them. The Lord our God made a covenant with us in Horeb. Not with our fathers did the Lord make this covenant, but with us, who are all of us here alive this day. The Lord spoke with you face to face at the mountain, out of the midst of the fire, while I stood between the Lord and you at the time, to declare to you the word of the Lord; for you were afraid because of the fire, and you did not go up into the mountain. He said: "I am the Lord your God, who brought you out of the land of Egypt, out of the house of bondage."

You shall have no other gods before me.

You shall not make for yourself a graven image or any likeness of anything that is in heaven above, or that is on the earth beneath, or that is in the water under the earth; you shall not bow down to them or serve them; for I the Lord your God am a jealous God, visiting the iniquity of the fathers upon the children to the third and fourth generation of those who hate me, but showing steadfast love to thousands of those who love me and keep my commandments.

You shall not take the name of the Lord your God in vain: for the Lord will not hold him guiltless who take his name in vain.

Observe the Sabbath day, to keep it holy, as the Lord your God commanded you. Six days you shall labor, and do all your work; but the seventh day is a Sabbath to the Lord your God; in it you shall not do any work, you or your son, or your daughter, or your manservant, or your maidservant, or your ox, or your ass, or any of your cattle, or the sojourner who is within your gates, that your manservant and your maidservant may rest as well as you. You shall remember that you were a servant in the land of Egypt, and the Lord your God brought you out thence with a mighty hand and an outstretched arm; therefore the Lord your God commanded you to keep the Sabbath day.

Honor your father and your mother as the Lord your God commanded you; that your days may be prolonged, and that it may go well with you, in the land which the Lord your God gives you.

You shall not kill.

Neither shall you commit adultery.

Neither shall you steal.

Neither shall you bear false witness against your neighbor.

Neither shall you covet your neighbor's wife; and you shall not desire your neighbor's house, his field, or his manservant, or his maidservant, his ox, or his ass, or anything that is your neighbor's.

These words the Lord spoke to all your assembly at the mountain out of the midst of the fire, the cloud, and the thick darkness, with a loud voice; and he added no more. And he wrote them upon two tables of stones, gave them to me....

Then Moses and the elders of Israel charged all the people as follows: Keep the entire commandment that I am commanding you today. On the day that you cross over the Jordan into the land that the LORD your God is giving you, you shall set up large stones and cover them with plaster. You shall write on them all the words of this law when you have crossed over, to enter the land that the LORD your God is giving you, a land flowing with milk and honey, as the LORD, the God of your ancestors, promised you. So when you have crossed over the Jordan, you shall set up these stones, about which I am commanding you today, on Mount Ebal, and you shall cover them with plaster. And you shall build an altar there to the LORD your God, an altar of stones on which you have not used an iron tool. You must build the altar of the LORD your God of unhewn stones. Then offer up burnt offerings on it to the LORD your God, make sacrifices of well-being, and eat them there, rejoicing before the LORD your God. You shall write on the stones all the words of this law very clearly.

Then Moses and the levitical priests spoke to all Israel, saying: Keep silence and hear, O Israel! This very day you have become the people of the LORD your God. Therefore obey the LORD your God, observing his commandments and his statutes that I am commanding you today.

The same day Moses charged the people as follows: When you have crossed over the Jordan, these shall stand on Mount Gerizim for the blessing of the people: Simeon, Levi, Judah, Issachar, Joseph, and Benjamin. And these shall stand on Mount Ebal for the curse: Reuben, Gad, Asher, Zebulun, Dan, and Naphtali. Then the Levites shall declare in a loud voice to all the Israelites:

"Cursed be anyone who makes an idol or casts an image, anything abhorrent to the LORD, the work of an artisan, and sets it up in secret." All the people shall respond, saying, "Amen!"

"Cursed be anyone who dishonors father or mother." All the people shall say, "Amen!"

"Cursed be anyone who moves a neighbor's boundary marker." All the people shall say, "Amen!"

The LORD spoke to Moses and Aaron, saying to them: Speak to the people of Israel, saying:

From among all the land animals, these are the creatures that you may eat. Any animal that has divided hoofs and is cleft-footed and chews the cud-such you may eat. But among those that chew the cud or have divided hoofs, you shall not eat the following: the camel, for even though it chews the cud, it does not have divided hoofs; it is unclean for you. The rock badger, for even though it chews the cud, it does not have divided hoofs; it is unclean for you. The hare, for even though it chews the cud, it does not have divided hoofs; it is unclean for you. The pig, for even though it has divided hoofs and is cleft-footed, it does not chew the cud; it is unclean for you.

Of their flesh you shall not eat, and their carcasses you shall not touch; they are unclean for you. These you may eat, of all that are in the waters. Everything in the waters that has fins and scales, whether in the seas or in the streams-such you may eat. But anything in the seas or the streams that does not have fins and scales, of the swarming creatures in the waters and among all the other living creatures that are in the waters-they are detestable to you and detestable they shall remain. Of their flesh you shall not eat, and their carcasses you shall regard as detestable. Everything in the waters that does not have fins and scales is detestable to you.

These you shall regard as detestable among the birds. They shall not be eaten; they are an abomination: the eagle, the vulture, the osprey, the buzzard, the kite of any kind; every raven of any kind; the ostrich, the nighthawk, the sea gull, the hawk of any kind; the little owl, the cormorant, the great owl, the water hen, the desert owl, the carrion vulture, the stork, the heron of any kind, the hoopoe, and the bat.

All winged insects that walk upon all fours are detestable to you. But among the winged insects that walk on all fours you may eat those that have jointed legs above their feet, with which to leap on the ground. Of them you may eat: the locust according to its kind, the bald locust according to its kind, the cricket according to its kind, and the grasshopper according to its kind. But all other winged insects that have four feet are detestable to you.

8.15 Absolute Monotheism

Thus says the LORD, the King of Israel,
and his Redeemer, the LORD of hosts:
I am the first and I am the last;
besides me there is no god.
Who is like me? Let them proclaim it,
let them declare and set it forth before me.
Who has announced from of old the
things to come?

Let them tell us what is yet to be.
Do not fear, or be afraid;
have I not told you from of old and
declared it?
You are my witnesses!
Is there any god besides me?
There is no other rock; I know not one.

All who make idols are nothing, and the things they delight in do not profit; their witnesses neither see nor know. And so they will be put to shame. Who would fashion a god or cast an image that can do no good? Look, all its devotees shall be put to shame; the artisans too are merely human. Let them all assemble, let them stand up; they shall be terrified, they shall all be put to shame.

The ironsmith fashions it and works it over the coals, shaping it with hammers, and forging it with his strong arm; he becomes hungry and his strength fails, he drinks no water and is faint. The carpenter stretches a line, marks it out with a stylus, fashions it with planes, and marks it with a compass; he makes it in human form, with human beauty, to be set up in a shrine. He cuts down cedars or chooses a holm tree or an oak and lets it grow strong among the trees of the forest. He plants a cedar and the rain nourishes it. Then it can be used as fuel. Part of it he takes and warms himself; he kindles a fire and bakes bread. Then he makes a god and worships it, makes it a carved image and bows down before it. Half of it he burns in the fire; over this half he roasts meat, eats it and is satisfied. He also warms himself and says, "Ah, I am warm, I can feel the fire!"

The rest of it he makes into a god, his idol, bows down to it and worships it; he prays to it and says, "Save me, for you are my god!"

They do not know, nor do they comprehend; for their eyes are shut, so that they cannot see, and their minds as well, so that they cannot understand. No one considers, nor is there knowledge or discernment to say, "Half of it I burned in the fire; I also baked bread on its coals, I roasted meat and have eaten. Now shall I make the rest of it an abomination? Shall I fall down before a block of wood?" He feeds on ashes; a deluded mind has led him astray, and he cannot save himself or say, "Is not this thing in my right hand a fraud?"

8.2   Selections from the Rabbinic Tradition

8.21   Selections from the Talmund

MISHNA A.

Moses received the Law on Sinai and delivered it to Joshua; Joshua in turn handed it down to the Elders (not to the seventy Elders of Moses' time but to the later Elders who have ruled Israel, and each of them delivered it to his successor); from the Elders it descended to the prophets (beginning with Eli and Samuel), and each of them delivered it to his successors until it reached the men of the Great Assembly. The last, named originated three maxims: "Be not hasty in judgment; Bring up many disciples; and, Erect safe guards for the Law."

Tosephhta—Aboth of R. Nathan.

Moses was sanctified in the cloud, and received the Torah from Sinai, as it is written [Ex. xxiv. 16]: "And the glory of the Lord abode upon Mount Sinai," which means on *Moses* (for what purpose?), to purify him; this occurred after the ten commandments had been given. So says R. Jose the Galilean; R. Aqiba, however, says: It is written [ibid.]: "And the cloud covered it six days." This refers to the *mountain*, before the ten commandments had been given, and this is what is written further on [ibid.]: "And he called unto Moses the seventh day out of the cloud" (for what purpose?—only) to confer honor upon him.

Said R. Nathan: Why did Moses stay the entire six days without communication from the Shekhina? To cleanse his body of all the food and drink it contained, that he might be like angels at the time of his consecration.

Said R. Mathia b. Heresh to him: Rabbi, all this stated above was done only to overawe him, that he might receive the words of the Torah with awe, terror, fear and trembling, as it is written [Ps. ii. "Serve the Lord with fear and rejoice with trembling."

It happened that R. Josiah and R. Mathia b. Heresh were both sitting and studying the Law. R. Josiah then departed to attend to worldly affairs. Said R. Mathia to him: "Rabbi, what dost thou gain by forsaking the words of the living God, and devoting thyself to worldly affairs? Even though thou art my master, and I thy disciple, yet I dare say that it is not right to do so." (Lest one say that R. Josiah did so from jealousy,) it was said: While sitting and studying the Torah they were jealous of each other, but when they parted they were like friends from youth.

Through Moses the Torah was given on Sinai, as it is written [Deut. v. 19]: "And he wrote them on two tables of stone, and he gave them unto me." And also [Lev. xxvi. 46]: "These are the statutes and ordinances and laws, which the Lord made between him and the children of Israel on Mount Sinai, by the hand of Moses." The Law which the Holy One, blessed be He, has given to Israel, was given only in the hand of Moses, as it is written [Ex. xxxi. 17]: "Between me and the children of Israel." So Moses (because of his purification and sanctification) was privileged to be the representative of Israel before the Lord.

Moses offered the ram of consecration and prepared the oil of anointment, and anointed therewith Aaron and his sons during all the seven days of consecration. With the same oil high-priests and kings were afterward anointed, and Elazar burned the (first) red-cow, with the ashes of which the unclean were purified in later generations. Said R. Eliezer: "The oil of anointment was of such importance that it remained even for the later generations, for Aaron and his *sons* were consecrated with the oil of anointment, as it is written [Ex. xxx. 30]: 'And Aaron and his sons shalt thou anoint, and consecrate them to be priests.'" (Hence we see that although Aaron was a high-priest, his sons, nevertheless, stood in need of anointment.)

Joshua received it (the Law) from Moses, as it is written [Numb. xxvii. 20]: "And thou shalt put some of thy greatness upon him, in order that all the congregation of the children of Israel may be obedient." The elders (who lived after Moses) received it from Joshua, as it is written [Judges ii. 7]: "And the people served the Lord all the days of Joshua, and all the days of the elders that lived many days after Joshua, who had seen all the great deeds of the Lord, which he had done for Israel." The judges received it from the elders, as it is written [Ruth, i. 1]: "And it came to pass in the days when the judges judged." 1 The prophets received it from the judges (beginning with Samuel the prophet, who was also a judge), as it is written [Jerem. vii. 25]: "And I sent unto you *all* my servants the prophets, sending them daily in the morning early." Haggai, Zechariah, and Malachi received it from the prophets. The men of the Great Assembly received it from. Haggai, Zechariah, and Malachi, and they said the following three things mentioned in the Mishna:

"Be deliberate in judgement." How so? It means a man shall be slow in his judgment, for he who is slow is deliberate, as it is written [Prov. xxv. 1]: "Also these are the proverbs of Solomon, which the men of Hezekiah the king of Judah have collected." They have not collected them,, but they were deliberating upon them before (making them public). Abba Saul, however, said: "Not only were they deliberating over them, but they also explained them."

Formerly it was said: The books of Proverbs, Song of Songs, and Ecclesiastes were hidden, because they are only parables, and do not belong to the Hagiographa; the men of the Great Assembly, however, came and explained them, as it is written [Prov. vii. 7-20]: "And I beheld among the simple ones, I discerned among the youths, a lad void of sense, etc. and, behold, a woman came to meet him with the attire of a harlot and obdurate of heart; she is noisy and ungovernable; in her house her feet never rest; at one time she is in the street, at another in the open places, and near every corner doth she lurk, and she caught hold of him, and kissed him, and with an impudent face she said to him, 'I had bound myself to bring peace-offerings; this day have I paid my vows; therefore I am come forth to meet thee, to seek thy presence diligently, and I have found thee. With tapestry coverings have I decked my bed, with embroidered coverlids of the fine linen of Egypt. I have sprinkled my couch with myrrh, aloes, and cinnamon. Come, let us indulge in love until the morning: let us delight ourselves with dalliances. For the man is not in his house, he is gone on a journey a great way off; the bag of money hath he taken with him; by the day of the new-moon festival only will he come home.'" And it is written also in Song of Songs [vii. 12, 13]: "Come, my friend, let us go into the field; let us spend the night in the villages; let us get up early to the vineyards; let us see if the wine have blossomed, whether the young grape have opened (to the view), whether the pomegranate have budded: there will I give my caresses unto thee." And it is written again in Ecclesiastes [xi. 9]: "Rejoice, O young man, in thy childhood; and let thy heart cheer thee in the days of thy youthful vigor, and walk firmly in the ways of thy heart, and in (the direction which) thy eyes see; but know thou, that concerning all these things God will bring thee into judgment." And again in Song of Songs [vii. 10]: "I am my friend's, and toward me is his desire." So we see that the last-mentioned passage of the Song of Songs explains all that was mentioned above; under the term "my friend's" the Lord is understood. Hence (it is sure) that they were not only deliberating, but also explaining them.

According to others the statement "Be deliberate in judgment means to teach that one shall be careful with his words, and also not to have an irascible manner against those who have received his words, for one who is easily provoked by those who have received his words often forgets his (original) words; for so we find with Moses, our master, who had forgotten his (original) words. (See Pesachim, p. 129: "Resh Lakish said," etc.)

And where do we find that Moses was irascible with his hearers? It is written [Numb. xxxi. 14]: "And Moses was wroth. . . . Have you allowed all the females to live?" And it is written: "Behold . . . through the counsel of Bil'am." How so? Infer from this that this was the advice of Bil'am given to Balak: "These people, your enemies, are hungry for food and are thirsty for drink, as they have nothing but manna. Go and put up tents for them, place in them food and drink, and seat in them beautiful women, daughters of nobles, so that the people may turn to Baal Peor." (This will be given in Sanhedrin in detail.)

Now from this we may draw an *a fortiori* conclusion. If Moses our master, the wisest of the wise and the father of the prophets, at the time he became angry at his listeners forgot his original words, so much the more would we commoners. From this we should learn how necessary it is to be careful and not irascible.

BABYLONIAN TALMUD translated by MICHAEL L. RODKINSON Book 5 (Vols. IX and X) [1918] Tracts Aboth, Derech Eretz-Rabba, Eretz-Zuta, and Baba Kama (First Gate)   http://www.sacred-texts.com/jud/t05/abo05.htm

8.22   Selections from the Midrash

1.1 Genesis 1:1ff., Part I

(Gen. 1:1:) IN THE BEGINNING GOD CREATED THE HEAVENS AND THE EARTH. It is written (in Ps. 104:3): WHO ROOFS HIS UPPER ROOMS IN THE WATERS, WHO SETS THE CLOUDS AS HIS CHARIOT.... R. Johanan said: Heaven and earth were created on the first day, and on the second the Holy One created the firmament and the angels. Where is it shown that they were created on the second day? Where it is stated (ibid.): WHO ROOFS HIS UPPER ROOMS IN THE WATERS, WHO SETS THE CLOUDS AS HIS CHARIOT, WHO WALKS ON THE WINGS OF THE WIND (*ruah*). And what is written next (in vs. 4)? WHO MAKES HIS ANGELS SPIRITS (*ruah*). R. Hanina said: The angels were created on the fifth day. Thus it is written concerning the fifth (in Gen. 1:20): AND LET FOWL FLY (*ye'ofef*) ABOVE THE EARTH. Now the word *ye'ofef* only refers to the flying of angels, as it is used (in Is. 6:2): AND WITH TWO HE DID FLY (*ye'ofef*). And why were the angels not created on the first day? So chat the heretics (*minim*) would not say: Michael was standing in the north with Gabriel in the south, and together they spread out the heavens and the earth. So who did create them? The Holy One by himself, as stated (in Gen. 1:1): IN THE BEGINNING GOD CREATED <THE HEAV-

ENS AND THE EARTH>. R. Judah and R. Nehemiah disagree. R. Judah says: The world was being created for six days. Thus it is written concerning the work of each and every day (in Gen. 1:7, 9, 11, 15, 24, 30): AND IT WAS SO. That is R. Judah's opinion, but R. Nehemiah says: The whole world was created on the first day. R. Judah said to him: What is the meaning of what is written concerning the work of each and every day: [AND IT WAS SO]? R. Berekhyah said concerning R. Nehemiah's opinion: (According to Gen. 1:24) GOD SAID: LET THE EARTH BRING FORTH. The expression LET BRING FORTH is only used of something that was prepared from IN THE BEGINNING, as stated concerning the first day (in vs. 1): IN THE BEGINNING.

8.23   Selections from the Mishnah

The Passover Seder

They mixed for him the first cup [of wine]: The House of Shammai say, "He says the blessing over the day and afterwards [he] says the blessing over the wine." And the House of Hillel say, "He says the blessing over the wine and afterwards [he] says the blessing over the day."

They served him: He dips the lettuce [the vegetable used for the bitter herbs] before he reached the bread condiment. They served him unleavened bread and lettuce and *haroset* [a mixture, e.g. of nuts, fruit, and wine pounded together] even though the *haroset* is not a [biblical] commandment. Rabbi Eleazar ben Zadok says, "It is a [biblical] commandment. And in the Temple they serve him the carcass of the Passover offering.

They poured for him the second cup, and here the child asks-and if the child lacks intelligence, his father instructs him-"How is this night different from all the [other] nights? For on all the [other] nights we eat leavened and unleavened bread, this night we eat only unleavened. For on all the [other] nights we eat other vegetables, on this night, *maror* (bitter herbs). For on all the [other] nights we eat meat roasted, steamed, or cooked [in a liquid, boiled], this night only [or 'all of it'] roasted. For on all the [other] nights we dip once, this night twice." According to the child's intelligence, his father instructs him. He starts [reading] with the disgrace [section of the Bible] and ends with the glory; and he expounds [the biblical section] from "A wandering Aramean was my father" (Deut. 26:5) until he finishes the entire portion.

Rabban Gamaliel said, "Whoever did not say these three things on Passover did not fulfill his obligation: *pesah, matzah,* and *merorim* [the Passover offering, unleavened bread, and bitter herbs]. *Pesah*-because the Omnipresent skipped over the houses of our ancestors in Egypt. *Merorim*-because the Egyptians embittered the lives of our ancestors in Egypt. *Matzah*-because they were redeemed. Therefore we are obligated to give thanks, to praise, to glorify, to crown, to exalt, to elevate the One who did for us all these miracles and took us out of slavery to freedom, and let us say before Him, Hallelujah" (Ps. 113:1ff.).

Up to what point does he recite [the Hallel]? The House of Shammai say, "Until '[He sets the childless woman among her household] as a happy mother of children' [the end of Ps. 113]." And the House of Hillel say, "Until '[Tremble ... at the presence of the Lord ... who turned] the flinty rock into a fountain' [the end of Ps. 124]." And [he] concludes with [the prayer for] "redemption." Rabbi Tarfon says, "...Who has redeemed us and redeemed our ancestors from Egypt and brought us to this night [to eat thereon unleavened bread and bitter herbs]"-and [he] does not conclude [with a concluding formula].

Rabbi Akiva says, "[One adds to the blessing:] Thus O Lord, our God and God of our ancestors, bring us in peace to the approaching festivals which are coming to meet us, rejoicing in the building of Your city and joyous in Your service, and to eat from the Passover and festive offerings the blood of which will reach the wall of Your altar with favor, and let us thank You for our redemption. Praised art Thou, Lord, Who redeemed Israel."

[They] poured for him the third cup [of wine]-he says the blessing over his food. [At] the fourth [cup], he finishes the Hallel [through Ps. 118], and says over it the blessing over the song. Between the former cups, if he wants to drink [further] he may drink. Between the third and fourth, he should not drink. After [eating from] the Passover offering, they do not end [with] *afiqomon* [revelry].

[If they] fell asleep: [if it was] some of them, they may eat [again because the remaining individuals of the group, who stayed awake, maintained the group]; and [if] all of them [fell asleep], [they] may not eat [again]. Rabbi Yose says, "If they dozed, they may eat [again]. And if they slumbered, [they] may not eat [again]."

After midnight the Passover offering imparts uncleanness to the hands; *piggul* [the "offensive" sacrifice] and *notar* [the "remnant"] impart uncleanness to the hands. [If one] said the blessing over the Passover offering, one is exempt from that over the festive offering; [if one said] the [blessing] over the festive offering, one is not exempt from that over the Passover offering"-the words of Rabbi Ishmael. Rabbi Akiva says, "[Saying] the former does not exempt [one from saying] the latter, and [saying] the latter does not exempt [one from saying] the former."

8.24   Selections from the Halakhah

Raising Together Diverse Species of Plants

A. Plants That Are or Are Not Classified as Diverse Kinds

M. 8:1 Diverse kinds of seeds [two kinds of seeds growing together] are prohibited from being sown and being allowed to grow, but are permitted in respect to eating [one may eat the produce of the seeds], and all the more so in respect to benefit [one may profit from them].

M. 1:1 (1) Wheat and tares are not [considered] diverse kinds with one another. (2) Barley and two-rowed barley, (3) rice wheat and spelt, (4) a broad bean and a French vetch, (5) a red grass-pea and a grass-pea, (6) and a hyacinth bean and a Nile cow-pea, are not [considered] diverse kinds with one another.

T. 1:1 [Concerning] all of the pairs which the sages enumerated [cf. M. Kil. 1:1] - one kind with its own kind are not [considered] diverse kinds [when they grow] with one another. And [concerning] the rest of the wild vegetables and garden vegetables [cf. M. Kil. 1:2D] - one kind with its own kind are not [considered] diverse kinds [when they grow] with one another.

T. 1:14 He who sows something [i.e., a seed] which sprouts [by nature], [either] over swamps or over rushes, is liable. [If he sows it] over a rock or over a water channel, he is free of liability. And [he who sows] something [i.e., a seed] which does not sprout [by nature], whether over swamps, or over rushes, or over, a water channel, is free of liability.

M. 1:2 A chatemelon and a muskmelon are not [considered] diverse kinds with one another. Lettuce and hill lettuce, chicories and wild chicories, leeks and wild leeks, coriander and wild coriander, mustard and Egyptian mustard, and an Egyptian gourd and a *remusah*, and a cow-pea and an asparagus bean, are not [considered] diverse kinds with one another.

8.3   A 16th Century Jewish Sermon

[We read] in the Midrash [cf. Ruth Rabbah 5:4]: "R. Abin said, There are wings to the earth, wings to the dawn, wings to the sun, wings to the cherubim, wings to the seraphim. Wings to the earth: *Have you seized the wings of the earth?* (Job 38:18); wings to the dawn: *If I take the wings of the dawn* (Ps. 139:9); wings to the sun: *the sun of righteousness, with healing in its wings* (Mal. 3:20); wings to the cherubim: *the sound of the wings of the cherubim* (Ezek. 10:5); wings to the seraphim: *each one had six wings* (Isa. 6:2). Great is the power of those who toil in Torah and those who perform acts of kindness, for they find shelter not in the shadow of the wings of the earth, or of the dawn, or of the sun, or of the cherubim or seraphim. In whose shadow do they find shelter? In the shadow of the One at whose word the world was created, as it is said, *How precious is Your lovingkindness, O God! Human beings find shelter in the shadow of Your wings* (Ps. 36:8)."

Yesterday we began to reveal the great and powerful benefit attainable in no other way than through devotion to the Torah. Let us now pass to a theoretical investigation of this matter, to be taken as far as the subject allows, and then supplement it with hidden content of mighty statements from the rabbis and the Bible.

Reason and logic make it clear to all that nourishment must befit the nature of that which is to be nourished. Now just as this is true for the body and its physical nourishment, so is it true for the rational soul: it is nourished and sustained by that which characteristically pertains to the intellect alone. But the rational soul is derived from the realm of the supernal and eternal beings. Just as they are nourished and sustained in life with nourishment befitting their nature by the rational apprehension of their Creator, so the rational soul must receive its nourishment and life-giving sustenance from this same source. None other will do.

As we now search through the various philosophical disciplines, the correctness of my premise will be established. Do you not see that the propaedeutic disciplines cannot possibly serve as nourishment befitting the vital sustenance of the rational soul? Their subject matter depends entirely upon things conceived by the intellect that have no reality outside the mind, things that are intellectually abstracted from matter, both ontologically and categorically. In this sense they do not really exist. Nor can the natural sciences, for their subject matter is constantly changing.

Nor can that which is called in philosophy "the divine science," that is, metaphysics, for theoretical investigation in this realm is merely wild speculation and surmise fraught with doubt, as its practitioners themselves concede. Further proof of this is the variety of incompatible views on basic questions. And even that which they are able to apprehend through their rational investigation is but *base silver laid over earthenware* (Prov. 26:23), for although they acknowledge the existence of a First Cause, they have *ardent lips with an evil mind* in associating the Name of God with something totally different, from which, as they assert, everything results by necessity. In short, all of the disciplines of human learning are inadequate as sources of vital sustenance for the rational soul.

This is not true of the divine Torah. Its subject matter is the creation of the world, the wondrous works of the One who is perfect in knowledge: pure intelligible ideas, capable of fully satisfying the rational soul with appropriate nourishment. Thus the benefit to be derived from the Torah, great and powerful, is unattainable from any other source. This is the meaning of the verse, *For man does not live by bread alone, but by all that issues from the mouth of the Lord* (Deut. 8:3). As the human being is composed of body and soul, there must be a special kind of nourishment for each part. Bread, composed of the [physical] elements, befits the body, which is also composed of them. But *that which issues from the mouth of the Lord* befits the rational part, for God has made one correspond to the other for our perpetual good.

As for the way in which this important doctrine is taught by the sages, consider the statement with which I began as an introduction to my message. Even though many have perused it, all reflecting their own concerns, there is still room left for me to express my view, although its value may be no greater in relation to the others than a single point is to the circumference.

You recall the various levels of being: inanimate, vegetative, animal, rational. All are natural. The intellect acquired by apprehending the disciplines of learning is left within the realm of human choice: human beings may make it fully actual. The people of Israel have yet another soul, from the soul of God on high, whose light shines over their heads.

Christianity

9.1   Selections from the New Testament

9.11   John the Baptist

In those days John the Baptist appeared in the wilderness of Judea, proclaiming, "Repent, for the kingdom of heaven has come near." This is the one of whom the prophet Isaiah spoke when he said,

> "The voice of one crying out in the wilderness:
> 'Prepare the way of the Lord, make his paths straight.

Now John wore clothing of camel's hair with a leather belt around his waist, and his food was locusts and wild honey. Then the people of Jerusalem and all Judea were going out to him, and all the region along the Jordan, and they were baptized by him in the river Jordan, confessing their sins.

But when he saw many Pharisees and Sadducees coming for baptism, he said to them, "You brood of vipers! Who warned you to flee from the wrath to come? Bear fruit worthy of repentance. Do not presume to say to yourselves, 'We have Abraham as our ancestor'; for I tell you, God is able from these stones to raise up children to Abraham. Even now the ax is lying at the root of the trees; every tree therefore that does not bear good fruit is cut down and thrown into the fire.

"I baptize you with water for repentance, but one who is more powerful than I is coming after me; I am not worthy to carry his sandals. He will baptize you with the Holy Spirit and fire. His winnowing fork is in his hand, and he will clear his threshing floor and will gather his wheat into the granary; but the chaff he will burn with unquenchable fire."

Then Jesus came from Galilee to John at the Jordan, to be baptized by him. John would have prevented him, saying, "I need to be baptized by you, and do you come to me?" But Jesus answered him, "Let it be so now; for it is proper for us in this way to fulfill all righteousness." Then he consented. And when Jesus had been baptized, just as he came up from the water, suddenly the heavens were opened to him and he saw the Spirit of God descending like a dove and alighting on him. And a voice from heaven said, "This is my Son, the Beloved, with whom I am well pleased."

Then Jesus was led up by the Spirit into the wilderness to be tempted by the devil. He fasted forty days and forty nights, and afterwards he was famished. The tempter came and said to him, "If you are the Son of God, command these stones to become loaves of bread." But he answered, "It is written, 'One does not live by bread alone, but by every word that comes from the mouth of God.

Then the devil took him to the holy city and placed him on the pinnacle of the temple, saying to him, "If you are the Son of God, throw yourself down; for it is written, 'He will command his angels concerning you,' and 'On their hands they will bear you up, so that you will not dash your foot against a stone.'"

Jesus said to him, "Again it is written, 'Do not put the Lord your God to the test.

Again, the devil took him to a very high mountain and showed him all the kingdoms of the world and their splendor; and he said to him, "All these I will give you, if you will fall down and worship me." Jesus said to him, "Away with you, Satan! for it is written, 'Worship the Lord your God, and serve only him.

Then the devil left him, and suddenly angels came and waited on him.

Now when Jesus heard that John had been arrested, he withdrew to Galilee. He left Nazareth and made his home in Capernaum by the sea, in the territory of Zebulun and Naphtali, so that what had been spoken through the prophet Isaiah might be fulfilled:

"Land of Zebulun, land of Naphtali,
on the road by the sea, across the Jordan, Galilee of the Gentiles—
the people who sat in darkness have seen a great light,
and for those who sat in the region and shadow of death light has dawned."

From that time Jesus began to proclaim, "Repent, for the kingdom of heaven has come near."

9.12   The Sermon on the Mount

As he walked by the Sea of Galilee, he saw two brothers, Simon, who is called Peter, and Andrew his brother, casting a net into the sea-for they were fishermen. And he said to them, "Follow me, and I will make you fish for people." Immediately they left their nets and followed him. As he went from there, he saw two other brothers, James son of Zebedee and his brother John, in the boat with their father Zebedee, mending their nets, and he called them. Immediately they left the boat and their father, and followed him.

Jesus went throughout Galilee, teaching in their synagogues and proclaiming the good news of the kingdom and curing every disease and every sickness among the people. So his fame spread throughout all Syria, and they brought to him all the sick, those who were afflicted with various diseases and pains, demoniacs, epileptics, and paralytics, and he cured them. And great crowds followed him from Galilee, the Decapolis, Jerusalem, Judea, and from beyond the Jordan.

When Jesus saw the crowds, he went up the mountain; and after he sat down, his disciples came to him. Then he began to speak, and taught them, saying:

"Blessed are the poor in spirit, for theirs is the kingdom of heaven.

"Blessed are those who mourn, for they will be comforted.

"Blessed are the meek, for they will inherit the earth.

"Blessed are those who hunger and thirst for righteousness, for they will be filled.

"Blessed are the merciful, for they will receive mercy.

"Blessed are the pure in heart, for they will see God.

"Blessed are the peacemakers, for they will be called children of God.

"Blessed are those who are persecuted for righteousness' sake, for theirs is the kingdom of heaven.

"Blessed are you when people revile you and persecute you and utter all kinds of evil against you falsely on my account. Rejoice and be glad, for your reward is great in heaven, for in the same way they persecuted the prophets who were before you.

"You are the salt of the earth; but if salt has lost its taste, how can its saltiness be restored? It is no longer good for anything, but is thrown out and trampled under foot.

"You are the light of the world. A city built on a hill cannot be hid. No one after lighting a lamp puts it under the bushel basket, but on the lampstand, and it gives light to all in the house. In the same way, let your light shine before others, so that they may see your good works and give glory to your Father in heaven.

"Do not think that I have come to abolish the law or the prophets; I have come not to abolish but to fulfill. For truly I tell you, until heaven and earth pass away, not one letter, not one stroke of a letter, will pass from the law until all is accomplished. Therefore, whoever breaks one of the least of these commandments, and teaches others to do the same, will be called least in the kingdom of heaven; but whoever does them and teaches them will be called great in the kingdom of heaven. For I tell you, unless your righteousness exceeds that of the scribes and Pharisees, you will never enter the kingdom of heaven.

"You have heard that it was said to those of ancient times, 'You shall not murder'; and 'whoever murders shall be liable to judgment.' But I say to you that if you are angry with a brother or sister, you will be liable to judgment; and if you insult a brother or sister, you will be liable to the council; and if you say, 'You fool,' you will be liable to the hell of fire. So when you are offering your gift at the altar, if you remember that your brother or sister has something against you, leave your gift there before the altar and go; first be reconciled to your brother or sister, and then come and offer your gift. Come to terms quickly with your accuser while you are on the way to court with him, or your accuser may hand you over to the judge, and the judge to the guard, and you will be thrown into prison.

Truly I tell you, you will never get out until you have paid the last penny.

"You have heard that it was said, 'You shall not commit adultery.' But I say to you that everyone who looks at a woman with lust has already committed adultery with her in his heart. If your right eye causes you to sin, tear it out and throw it away; it is better for you to lose one of your members than for your whole body to be thrown into hell. And if your right hand causes you to sin, cut it off and throw it away; it is better for you to lose one of your members than for your whole body to go into hell.

"It was also said, 'Whoever divorces his wife, let him give her a certificate of divorce.' But I say to you that anyone who divorces his wife, except on the ground of unchastity, causes her to commit adultery; and whoever marries a divorced woman commits adultery.

"Again, you have heard that it was said to those of ancient times, 'You shall not swear falsely, but carry out the vows you have made to the Lord.' But I say to you, Do not swear at all, either by heaven, for it is the throne of God, or by the earth, for it is his footstool, or by Jerusalem, for it is the city of the great King. And do not swear by your head, for you cannot make one hair white or black. Let your word be 'Yes, Yes' or 'No, No'; anything more than this comes from the evil one.

"You have heard that it was said, 'An eye for an eye and a tooth for a tooth.' But I say to you, Do not resist an evildoer. But if anyone strikes you on the right cheek, turn the other also; and if anyone wants to sue you and take your coat, give your cloak as well; and if anyone forces you to go one mile, go also the second mile. Give to everyone who begs from you, and do not refuse anyone who wants to borrow from you.

"You have heard that it was said, 'You shall love your neighbor and hate your enemy.' But I say to you, Love your enemies and pray for those who persecute you, to that you may be children of your Father in heaven; for he makes his sun rise on the evil and on the good, and sends rain on the righteous and on the unrighteous. For if you love those who love you, what reward do you have? Do not even the tax collectors do the same? And if you greet only your brothers and sisters,f what more are you doing than others? Do not even the Gentiles do the same? Be perfect, therefore, as your heavenly Father is perfect.

9.13   The Crucifiction and Resurrection

Two others also, who were criminals, were led away to be put to death with him. When they came to the place that is called The Skull, they crucified Jesus there with the criminals, one on his right and one on his left. Then Jesus said, "Father, forgive them; for they do not know what they are doing." And they cast lots to divide his clothing. And the people stood by, watching; but the leaders scoffed at him, saying, "He saved others; let him save himself if he is the Messiah of God, his chosen one!" The soldiers also mocked him, coming up and offering him sour wine, and saying; "If you are the King of the Jews, save yourself?" There was also an inscription over him, "This is the King of the Jews."

One of the criminals who were hanged there kept deriding him and saying "Are you not the Messiah? Save yourself and us!" But the other rebuked him, saying, "Do you not fear God, since you are under the same sentence of condemnation? And we indeed have been condemned justly, for we are getting what we deserve for our deeds, but this man has done nothing wrong." Then he said, "Jesus, remember me when you come into your kingdom." He replied, "Truly I tell you, today you will be with me in Paradise."

It was now about noon, and darkness came over the whole land until three in the afternoon, while the sun's light failed; and the curtain of the temple was torn in two. Then Jesus, crying with a loud voice, said, "Father, into your hands I commend my spirit." Having said this, he breathed his last. When the centurion saw what had taken place, he praised God and said, "Certainly this man was innocent." And when all the crowds who had gathered there for this spectacle saw what had taken place, they returned home, beating their breasts. But all his acquaintances, including, the women who had followed him from Galilee, stood at a distance, watching these things.

But on the first day of the week, at early dawn, they came to the tomb, taking the spices that they had prepared. They found the stone rolled away from the tomb, but when they went in, they did not find the body. While they were perplexed about this, suddenly two men in dazzling clothes stood beside them. The women were terrified and bowed their faces to the ground, but the men said to them, "Why do you look for the living among the dead? He is not here, but has risen. Remember how he told you, while he was still in Galilee, that the Son of Man must be handed over to sinners, and be crucified, and on the third day rise again." Then they remembered his words, and returning from the tomb, they told all this to the eleven and to all the rest. Now it was Mary Magdalene, Joanna, Mary the mother of James, and the other women with them who told this to the apostles. But these words seemed to them an idle tale, and they did not believe them. But Peter got up and ran to the tomb; stooping and looking in, he saw the linen cloths by themselves; then he went home, amazed at what had happened.

9.2 Selections from *The Literal Meaning of Genesis* by Saint Augustine

Chapter V.—Concerning the Motives to Sin, Which are Not in the Love of Evil, But in the Desire of Obtaining the Property of Others.

10. There is a desirableness in all beautiful bodies, and in gold, and silver, and all things; and in bodily contact sympathy is powerful, and each other sense hath his

proper adaptation of body. Worldly honour hath also its glory, and the power of command, and of overcoming; whence proceeds also the desire for revenge. And yet to acquire all these, we must not depart from Thee, O Lord, nor deviate from Thy law. The life which we live here hath also its peculiar attractiveness, through a certain measure of comeliness of its own, and harmony with all things here below. The friendships of men also are endeared by a sweet bond, in the oneness of many souls. On account of all these, and such as these, is sin committed; while through an inordinate preference for these goods of a lower kind, the better and higher are neglected,—even Thou, our Lord God, Thy truth, and Thy law. For these meaner things have their delights, but not like unto my God, who hath created all things; for in Him doth the righteous delight, and He is the sweetness of the upright in heart.

11. When, therefore, we inquire why a crime was committed, we do not believe it, unless it appear that there might have been the wish to obtain some of those which we designated meaner things, or else a fear of losing them. For truly they are beautiful and comely, although in comparison with those higher and celestial goods they be abject and contemptible. A man hath murdered another; what was his motive? He desired his wife or his estate; or would steal to support himself; or he was afraid of losing something of the kind by him; or, being injured, he was burning to be revenged. Would he commit murder without a motive, taking delight simply in the act of murder? Who would credit it? For as for that savage and brutal man, of whom it is declared that he was gratuitously wicked and cruel, there is yet a motive assigned. "Lest through idleness," he says, "hand or heart should grow inactive." And to what purpose? Why, even that, having once got possession of the city through that practice of wickedness, he might attain unto honours, empire, and wealth, and be exempt from the fear of the laws, and his difficult circumstances from the needs of his family, and the consciousness of his own wickedness. So it seems that even Catiline himself loved not his own villanies, but something else, which gave him the motive for committing them.

Chapter VI.—Why He Delighted in that Theft, When All Things Which Under the Appearance of Good Invite to Vice are True and Perfect in God Alone.

12. What was it, then, that I, miserable one, so doted on in thee, thou theft of mine, thou deed of darkness, in that sixteenth year of my age? Beautiful thou wert not, since thou wert theft. But art thou anything, that so I may argue the case with thee? Those pears that we stole were fair to the sight, because they were Thy creation, Thou fairest of all, Creator of all, Thou good God—God, the highest good, and my true good. Those pears truly were pleasant to the sight; but it was not for them that my miserable soul lusted, for I had abundance of better, but those I plucked simply that I might steal. For, having plucked them, I threw them away, my sole gratification in them being my own sin, which I was pleased to enjoy. For if any of these pears entered my mouth, the sweetener of it was my sin in eating it. And now, O Lord my God, I ask what it was in that theft of mine that caused me such delight; and behold it hath no beauty in it—not such, I mean, as exists in justice and wisdom; nor such as is in the mind, memory, senses, and animal life of man; nor yet such as is the glory and beauty of the stars in their courses; or the earth, or the sea, teeming with incipi-

ent life, to replace, as it is born, that which decayeth; nor, indeed, that false and shadowy beauty which pertaineth to deceptive vices.

13. For thus doth pride imitate high estate, whereas Thou alone art God, high above all. And what does ambition seek but honours and renown, whereas Thou alone art to be honoured above all, and renowned for evermore? The cruelty of the powerful wishes to be feared; but who is to be feared but God only, out of whose power what can be forced away or withdrawn—when, or where, or whither, or by whom? The enticements of the wanton would fain be deemed love; and yet is naught more enticing than Thy charity, nor is aught loved more healthfully than that, Thy truth, bright and beautiful above all. Curiosity affects a desire for knowledge, whereas it is Thou who supremely knowest all things. Yea, ignorance and foolishness themselves are concealed under the names of ingenuousness and harmlessness, because nothing can be found more ingenuous than Thou; and what is more harmless, since it is a sinner's own works by which he is harmed?

And sloth seems to long for rest; but what sure rest is there besides the Lord? Luxury would fain be called plenty and abundance; but Thou art the fulness and unfailing plenteousness of unfading joys. Prodigality presents a shadow of liberality; but Thou art the most lavish giver of all good. Covetousness desires to possess much; and Thou art the Possessor of all things. Envy contends for excellence; but what so excellent as Thou? Anger seeks revenge; who avenges more justly than Thou? Fear starts at unwonted and sudden chances which threaten things beloved, and is wary for their security; but what can happen that is unwonted or sudden to Thee? or who can deprive Thee of what Thou lovest? or where is there unshaken security save with Thee? Grief languishes for things lost in which desire had delighted itself, even because it would have nothing taken from it, as nothing can be from Thee.

14. Thus doth the soul commit fornication when she turns away from Thee, and seeks without Thee what she cannot find pure and untainted until she returns to Thee. Thus all pervertedly imitate Thee who separate themselves far from Thee and raise themselves up against Thee. But even by thus imitating Thee they acknowledge Thee to be the Creator of all nature, and so that there is no place whither they can altogether retire from Thee. What, then, was it that I loved in that theft? And wherein did I, even corruptedly and pervertedly, imitate my Lord? Did I wish, if only by artifice, to act contrary to Thy law, because by power I could not, so that, being a captive, I might imitate an imperfect liberty by doing with impunity things which I was not allowed to do, in obscured likeness of Thy omnipotency? Behold this servant of Thine, fleeing from his Lord, and following a shadow! O rottenness! O monstrosity of life and profundity of death! Could I like that which was unlawful only because it was unlawful?

The Confessions and Letters of St. Augustin, with a Sketch of his Life and Work
Creator(s): Schaff, Philip (1819-1893) Print Basis: New York: Christian Literature Publishing Co., 1886 Rights: Public Domain
http://www.ccel.org/ccel/schaff/npnf101.txt

9.3 Selections From the Rule of Saint Benedict

LI S T E N carefully, my child,
to your master's precepts,
and incline the ear of your heart (Prov. 4:20).
Receive willingly and carry out effectively
your loving father's advice,
that by the labor of obedience
you may return to Him
from whom you had departed by the sloth of disobedience.

To you, therefore, my words are now addressed,
whoever you may be,
who are renouncing your own will
to do battle under the Lord Christ, the true King,
and are taking up the strong, bright weapons of obedience.

And first of all,
whatever good work you begin to do,
beg of Him with most earnest prayer to perfect it,
that He who has now deigned to count us among His children
may not at any time be grieved by our evil deeds.
For we must always so serve Him
with the good things He has given us,
that He will never as an angry Father disinherit His children,
nor ever as a dread Lord, provoked by our evil actions,
deliver us to everlasting punishment
as wicked servants who would not follow Him to glory.

Jan. 2 - May 3 - Sept. 2

Let us arise, then, at last,
for the Scripture stirs us up, saying,

"Now is the hour for us to rise from sleep" (Rom. 18:11).
Let us open our eyes to the deifying light,
let us hear with attentive ears
the warning which the divine voice cries daily to us,
"Today if you hear His voice,
harden not your hearts" (Ps. 94:8).
And again,
"Whoever has ears to hear,
hear what the Spirit says to the churches" (Matt. 11-15; Apoc. 2:7).
And what does He say?
"Come, My children, listen to Me;
I will teach you the fear of the Lord" (Ps. 33:12).
"Run while you have the light of life,
lest the darkness of death overtake you" (John 12:35).

Jan. 3 - May 4 - Sept. 3

And the Lord, seeking his laborer
in the multitude to whom He thus cries out,
says again,
"Who is the one who will have life,
and desires to see good days" (Ps. 33:13)?
And if, hearing Him, you answer,
"I am the one,"
God says to you,
"If you will have true and everlasting life,
keep your tongue from evil
and your lips that they speak no guile.
Turn away from evil and do good;
seek after peace and pursue it" (Ps. 33:14-15).
And when you have done these things,
My eyes shall be upon you
and My ears open to your prayers;
and before you call upon Me,

I will say to you,
'Behold, here I am'" (Ps. 33:16; Is. 65:24;
  58:9).
What can be sweeter to us, dear ones,
than this voice of the Lord inviting us?
Behold, in His loving kindness
the Lord shows us the way of life.

Jan. 4 - May 5 - Sept. 4

Having our loins girded, therefore,
with faith and the performance of good
  works (Eph. 6:14),
let us walk in His paths
by the guidance of the Gospel,
that we may deserve to see Him
who has called us to His kingdom (1
  Thess. 2:12).
For if we wish to dwell in the tent of that
  kingdom,
we must run to it by good deeds
or we shall never reach it.
But let us ask the Lord, with the
  Prophet,
"Lord, who shall dwell in Your tent,
or who shall rest upon Your holy mountain" (Ps. 14:1)?
After this question, brothers and sisters,
let us listen to the Lord
as He answers and shows us the way to
  that tent, saying,
"The one Who walks without stain and
  practices justice;
who speaks truth from his heart;
who has not used his tongue for deceit;
who has done no evil to his neighbor;
who has given no place to slander
  against his neighbor."

This is the one who,
under any temptation from the malicious devil,
has brought him to naught (Ps. 14:4)
by casting him and his temptation from
  the sight of his heart;
and who has laid hold of his thoughts
while they were still young
and dashed them against Christ (Ps.
  136:9).
It is they who,
fearing the Lord (Ps. 14:4),
do not pride themselves on their good
  observance;
but,
convinced that the good which is in
  them
cannot come from themselves and must
  be from the Lord,
glorify the Lord's work in them (Ps.
  14:4),
using the words of the Prophet,
"Not to us, O Lord, not to us,
but to Your name give the glory" (Ps.
  113, 2nd part:1).
Thus also the Apostle Paul
attributed nothing of the success of his
  preaching to himself,
but said,
"By the grace of God I am what I am" (1
  Cor. 15:10).
And again he says,
"He who glories, let him glory in the
  Lord" (2 Cor. 10:17).

The Order of St. Benedict
www.osb.org/rb/text/rbejms1.html

9.4   "To the Bishops of Sardinia."

Selections from a Letter from Pope Clement XIV

To the Bishops of Sardinia.
Venerable Brethren, Greetings and Apostolic Blessing.

It is altogether befitting for the ministers of the Church and the dispensers of divine mysteries to be exempt from any suspicion, however light, of avarice; then they can be free to exercise their sacred ministry in such a way that they can justly glory that their hands have acted free of any reward. In fact Christ ordered this when He sent His disciples to preach the gospel with the words, "Freely give what you have freely received" (Mt 18.8). Paul also stated (1 Tm 3.8; Ti 1.7) that this should be required of those chosen for the ministry of the altar. This, finally, Peter inculcated in those in charge of the care of souls, saying, "Be shepherds of the flock of God entrusted to you, watching over it not for sordid gain, but freely" (1 Pt 5.2).

Pastors of the Church, who ought to be an example to the faithful, must diligently observe this divine command and thus show themselves irreprehensible; they must also be vigilant so as not to permit the lower ministers over whom they have charge to perpetrate anything to the contrary. They should always remember that noble sentiment of Ambrose (Commentary on Lk 4.52), "Nevertheless, it is not sufficient if you yourselves do not seek profit: the hands of your household must also be restrained. Therefore instruct your household, exhort and watch over it: and if your servant deceive you, let him be repudiated, if apprehended, as scripture instructs."

Accordingly, both the holy councils and previous Roman Pontiffs have repeatedly advocated that every possible avenue be closed so that such evil abuses never creep into the Church of God, or if, by chance, they had already done so, they be totally eradicated from its midst. It is lamentable that these sanctions have either lacked effect in some dioceses or been insufficiently strong or valid enough to root out totally all contrary usages. And We know that this has come about because those whose duty it was to carry them out most strictly have put forward various excuses, such as ancient and inveterate custom or the need of bestowing some reward on the ministers of ecclesiastical curias or the necessity of making up for the lack of the means of support required for a proper and decent manner of living in keeping with one's state.

Because he understood all this properly, Innocent XI, desiring to invalidate any excuses whatsoever, in 1678 ordered that everything pertinent to the matter be collected from the sacred canons, the Council of Trent, the interpretations given by the congregations of this Council, and proposals from consultations with bishops. Furthermore he ordered that an explicit determination and mention by name be made of all ecclesiastical affairs for which the reception of any payment on the part of ecclesiastical courts and episcopal curias was forbidden. The sole exception concerned what ought to go to the Chancellor alone as a proper remuneration or as a necessary payment. The same document also provided that in these matters the same procedure and uniform discipline be observed in all ecclesiastical curias; any custom to the contrary should be completely repudiated. Innocent XI approved and confirmed this on October first of the same year and ordered its promulgation and observance.

Nevertheless, not even this was enough to restore the univeral collapse of ecclesiastical discipline or to curb depraved customs rooted in various dioceses. One objection was that the aforesaid did not impose a law to be observed in ecclesiastical curias outside of Italy as well. Nonetheless the decrees contained in it were taken from sacred canons and principally from the Council of Trent, which all ecclesiastical curias must obey.

2. Accordingly, with sorrow We have learned that many abuses in the exercise of spiritual power (which not only totally destroy ecclesiastical discipline, but also enfeeble and bring the greatest shame upon your dignity and power) still exist in your ecclesiastical curias. To be sure your piety, your holy mode of life, your solicitude for your churches is more than sufficiently known to Us. We also know that these abuses have been introduced in the past, first from some secondary ministry or other, and have been gradually spread from diocese to diocese, perhaps without the knowledge of bishops. In certain places the greater dignity of a particular church has even led to the increase of such abuses. Some ministers, whose successors in office or ministry paid little attention and incautiously followed the footsteps of their own predecessors, deemed these long standing and customary abuses worthy of being proposed for approval by synodal constitutions. Accordingly, you can in no way be blamed; rather you are worthy of commendation because, as We have learned, you are grieved by these abuses and wish to extirpate them.

We, however, perceiving how much you will be detested for this and how great the obstacles will be unless the Apostolic Authority assists you in this enterprise, accordingly make this intervention. We do this especially because of the diversity of the fees and the varying practices in different dioceses. As a result of Our intervention, We anticipate conformity among all dioceses. Wherefore We are confident that you will faithfully carry out Our decrees which were requested by Charles Emmanuel, the illustrious king of Sardinia. We are also confident that you will see to it that they are diligently observed by all to whom they pertain.

Remuneration for Ordinations

3. First, as far as concerns holy orders, you can hardly be ignorant of the practically innumerable laws of the Church which forbid bishops and others ordaining or any officials to receive anything from conferring orders. This was most clearly forbidden by the Ecumenical Council of Chalcedon in 451 (canon 2), by the Roman Synod held under St. Gregory the great in 600 or 604 (canon 5) and elsewhere in his *Epistles* (bk. 4, epistle 44, indictment 13), by the Second Ecumenical Council of Nicaea in 787 (canon 5), by that of Pavia in 1022 (canon 3), by the Fourth Lateran Council under Innocent III in 1215, as well as by the councils of Tours, Braga and Barcelona, among

others (collected by Christia Wolf in *dissert. 2 proem. de simonia*, chap. 9, tome 4 and by Gonzales in chapter *Antequam I de simonia*, no.9), and, most recently, by the Council of Trent (session 21, chap. 1 on reform) which emended the ancient canons allowing a spontaneous offering to be accepted and restored ecclesiastical discipline concerning ordination to its pristine and ancient purity.

9.5   Martin Luther's Ninety-Five Theses

Out of love and zeal for truth and the desire to bring it to light, the following theses will be publicly discussed at Wittenberg under the chairmanship of the reverend father Martin Lutther, Master of Arts and Sacred Theology and regularly appointed Lecturer on these subjects at that place. He requests that those who cannot be present to debate orally with us will do so by letter.

In the Name of Our Lord Jesus Christ. Amen.

1. When our Lord and Master Jesus Christ said, "Repent" [Matt. 4:17], he willed the entire life of believers to be one of repentance.

2. This word cannot be understood as referring to the sacrament of penance, that is, confession and satisfaction, as administered by the clergy.

3. Yet it does not mean solely inner repentance; such inner repentance is worthless unless it produces various outward mortifications of the flesh.

4. The penalty of sin remains as long as the hatred of self, that is, true inner repentance, until our entrance into the kingdom of heaven.

5. The pope neither desires nor is able to remit any penalties except those imposed by his own authority or that of the canons.

6. The pope cannot remit any guilt, except by declaring and showing that it has been remitted by God; or, to be sure, by remitting guilt in cases reserved to his judgment. If his right to grant remission in these cases were disregarded, the guilt would certainly remain unforgiven.

7. God remits guilt to no one unless at the same time he humbles him in all things and makes him submissive to his vicar, the priest.

8. The penitential canons are imposed only on the living, and, according to the canons themselves, nothing should be imposed on the dying.

9. Therefore the Holy Spirit through the pope is kind to us insofar as the pope in his decrees always makes exception of the article of death and of necessity.

10. Those priests act ignorantly and wickedly who, in the case of the dying, reserve canonical penalties for purgatory.

11. Those tares of changing the canonical penalty to the penalty of purgatory were evidently sown while the bishops slept [Matt. 13:25].

12. In former times canonical penalties were imposed, not after, but before absolution, as tests of true contrition.

13. The dying are freed by death from all penalties, are already dead as far as the canon laws are concerned, and have a right to be released from them.

14. Imperfect piety or love on the part of the dying person necessarily brings with it great fear; and the smaller the love, the greater the fear.

15. This fear or horror is sufficient in itself, to say nothing of other things, to constitute the penalty of purgatory, since it is very near the horror of despair.

16. Hell, purgatory, and heaven seem to differ the same as despair, fear, and assurance of salvation.

17. It seems as though for the souls in purgatory fear should necessarily decrease and love increase.

18. Furthermore, it does not seem proved, either by reason or Scripture, that souls in purgatory are outside the state of merit, that is, unable to grow in love.

19. Nor does it seem proved that souls in purgatory, at least not all of them, are certain and assured of their own salvation, even if we ourselves may be entirely certain of it.

20. Therefore the pope, when he uses the words "plenary remission of all penalties," does not actually mean "all penalties," but only those imposed by himself.

21. Thus those indulgence preachers are in error who say that a man is absolved from every penalty and saved by papal indulgences.

22. As a matter of fact, the pope remits to souls in purgatory no penalty which, according to canon law, they should have paid in this life.

23. If remission of all penalties whatsoever could be granted to anyone at all, certainly it would be granted only to the most perfect, that is, to very few.

24. For this reason most people are necessarily deceived by that indiscriminate and high-sounding promise of release from penalty.

25. That power which the pope has in general over purgatory corresponds to the power which any bishop or curate has in a particular way in his own diocese or parish.

26. The pope does very well when he grants remission to souls in purgatory, not by the power of the keys, which he does not have, but by way of intercession for them.

27. They preach only human doctrines who say that as soon as the money clinks into the money chest, the soul flies out of purgatory.

28. It is certain that when money clinks in the money chest, greed and avarice can be increased; but when the church intercedes, the result is in the hands of God alone.

29. Who knows whether all souls in purgatory wish to be redeemed, since we have exceptions in St. Severinus and St. Paschal, as related in a legend.

30. No one is sure of the integrity of his own contrition, much less of having received plenary remission.

31. The man who actually buys indulgences is as rare as he who is really penitent; indeed, he is exceedingly rare.

32. Those who believe that they can be certain of their salvation because they have indulgence letters will be eternally damned, together with their teachers.

33. Men must especially be on their guard against those who say that the pope's pardons are that inestimable gift of God by which man is reconciled to him.

34. For the graces of indulgences are concerned only with the penalties of sacramental satisfaction. established by man.

35. They who teach that contrition is not necessary on the part of those who intend to buy souls out of purgatory or to buy confessional privileges preach unchristian doctrine.

36. Any truly repentant Christian has a right to full remission of penalty and guilt, even without indulgence letters.

37. Any true Christian, whether living or dead, participates in all the blessings of Christ and the church; and this is granted him by God, even without indulgence letters.

38. Nevertheless, papal remission and blessing are by no means to be disregarded, for they are, as I have said [Thesis 6], the proclamation of the divine remission.

39. It is very difficult, even for the most learned theologians, at one and the same time to commend to the people the bounty of indulgences and the need of true contrition.

40. A Christian who is truly contrite seeks and loves to pay penalties for his sins; the bounty of indilgences, however, causes men to hate them - at least it furnishes occasion for hating them.

41. Papal indulgences must be preached with caution, lest people erroneously think that they are preferable to other good works of love.

42. Christians are to be taught that the pope does not intend that the buying of indulgences should in any way be compared with works of mercy.

43. Christians are to be taught that he who gives to the poor or lends to the needy does a better deed than he who buys indulgences.

44. Because love grows by works of love, man thereby becomes better. Man does not, however, become better by means of indulgences but is merely freed from penalties.

45. Christians are to be taught that he who sees a needy man and passes him by, yet gives his money for indulgences, does not buy papal indulgences but God's wrath.

46. Christians are to be taught that, unless they have more than they need, they must reserve enough for their family needs and by no means squander it on indulgences.

47. Christians are to be taught that the buying of indulgences is a matter of free choice, not commanded.

48. Christians are to be taught that the pope, in granting indulgences, needs and thus desires their devout prayer more than their money.

49. Christians are to be taught that papal indulgences are useful only if they do not put their trust in them, but very harmful if they lose their fear of God because of them.

50. Christians are to be taught that if the pope knew the exactions of the indulgence preachers, he would rather that the basilica of St. Peter were burned to ashes than built up with the skin, flesh, and bones of his sheep.

51. Christians are to be taught that the pope would and should wish to give of his own money, even though he had to sell the basilica of St. Peter, to many of those from whom certain hawkers of indulgences cajole money.

52. It is vain to trust in salvation by indulgence letters, even though the indulgence commissary, or even the pope, were to offer his soul as security.

53. They are enemies of Christ and the pope who forbid altogether the preaching of the Word of God in some churches in order that indulgences may be preached in others.

54. Injury is done the Word of God when, in the same sermon, an equal or larger amount of time is devoted to indulgences than to the Word.

55. It is certainly the pope's sentiment that if indulgences, which are a very insignificant thing, are celebrated with one bell, one procession, and one ceremony, then the gospel, which is the very greatest thing, should be preached with a hundred bells, a hundred processions, a hundred ceremonies.

56. The treasures of the church, out of which the pope distributes indulgences, are not sufficiently discussed or known among the people of Christ.

57. That indulgences are not temporal treasures is certainly clear, for many [indulgence] preachers do not distribute them freely but only gather them.

58. Nor are they the merits of Christ and the saints, for, even without the pope, the latter always work grace for the inner man, and the cross, death, and hell for the outer man.

59. St. Laurence said that the poor of the church were the treasures of the church, but he spoke according to the usage of the word in his own time.

60. Without want of consideration we say that the keys of the church, given by the merits of Christ, are that treasure;

61. For it is clear that the pope's power is of itself sufficient for the remission of penalities and cases reserved by himself.

62. The true treasure of the church is the most holy gospel of the glory and grace of God.

63. But this treasure is naturally most odious, for it makes the first to be last [Matt. 20:16].

64. On the other hand, the treasure of indulgences is naturally most acceptable, for it makes the last to be first.

65. Therefore the treasures of the gospel are nets with which one formerly fished for men of wealth.

66. The treasures of indulgences are nets with which one now fishes for the wealth of men.

67. The indulgences which the demagogues acclaim as the greatest graces are actually understood to be such only insofar as they promote gain.

68. They are nevertheless in truth the most insignificant graces when compared with the grace of God and the piety of the cross.

69. Bishops and curates are bound to admit the commissaries of papal indulgences with all reverence.

70. But they are much more bound to strain their eyes and ears lest these men preach their own dreams instead of what the pope has commissioned.

71. Let him who speaks against the truth concerning papal indulgences be anathema and accursed;

72. But let him who guards against the lust and license of the indulgence preachers be blessed;

73. Just as the pope justly thunders against those who by any means whatsoever contrive harm to the sale of indulgences.

74. But much more does he intend to thunder against those who use indulgences as a pretext to contrive harm to holy love and truth.

75. To consider papal indulgences so great that they could absolve a man even if he had done the impossible and had violated the mother of God is madness.

76. We say on the contrary that papal indulgences cannot remove the very least of venial sins as far as guilt is concerned.

77. To say that even St. Peter, if he were now pope, could not grant greater graces is blasphemy against St. Peter and the pope.

78. We say on the contrary that even the present pope, or any pope whatsoever, has greater graces at his disposal, that is, the gospel, spiritual powers, gifts of healing, etc., as it is written in I Cor. 12 [:28].

79. To say that the cross emblazoned with the papal coat of arms, and set up by the indulgence preachers, is equal in worth to the cross of Christ is blasphemy.

80. The bishops, curates, and theologians who permit such talk to be spread among the people will have to answer for this.

81. This unbridled preaching of indulgences makes it difficult even for learned men to rescue the reverence which is due the pope from slander or from the shrewd questions of the laity,

82. Such as: "Why does not the pope empty purgatory for the sake of holy love and the dire need of the souls that are there if he redeems an infinite number of souls for the sake of miserable money with which to build a church? The former reasons would be most just; the latter is most trivial."

83. Again, "Why are funeral and anniversary masses for the dead continued and why does he not return or permit the withdrawal of the endowments founded for them, since it is wrong to pray for the redeemed?"

84. Again, "What is this new piety of God and the pope that for a consideration of money they permit a man who is impious and their enemy to buy out of purgatory the pious soul of a friend of God' and do not rather, because of the need of that pious and beloved soul, free it for pure love's sake?"

85. Again, "Why are the penitential canons, long since abrogated and dead in actual fact and through disuse, now satisfied by the granting of indulgences as though they were still alive and in force?"

86. Again, "Why does not the pope, whose wealth is today greater than the wealth of the richest Crassus, build this one basilica of St. Peter with his own money rather than with the money of poor believers?"

87. Again, "What does the pope remit or grant to those who by perfect contrition already have a right to full remission and blessings?"

88. Again, "What greater blessing could come to the church than if the pope were to bestow these remissions and blessings on every believer a hundred times a day, as he now does but once?"

89. "Since the pope seeks the salvation of souls rather than money by his indulgences, why does he suspend the indulgences and pardons previously granted when they have equal efficacy?"

90. To repress these very sharp arguments of the laity by force alone, and not to resolve them by giving reasons, is to expose the church and the pope to the ridicule of their enemies and to make Christians unhappy.

91. If, therefore, indulgences were preached according to the spirit and intention of the pope, all these doubts would be readily resolved. Indeed, they would not exist.

92. Away then with all those prophets who say to the people of Christ, "Peace, peace," and there is no peace! [Jer. 6:14] .

93. Blessed be all those prophets who say to the people of Christ, "Cross, cross," and there is no cross!

94. Christians should be exhorted to be diligent in following Christ, their head, through penalties, death, and hell;

95. And thus be confident of entering into heaven through many tribulations rather than through the false security of peace [Acts 14:22].

Islam

10.1   Selections from the Qur'an

10.11   The Opening

In the name of Allah, the Beneficent, the Merciful.
All praise is due to Allah, the Lord of the Worlds
The Beneficent, the Merciful.
Master of the Day of Judgment.
Thee do we serve and Thee do we beseech for help.
Keep us on the right path.
The path of those upon whom Thou hast bestowed favors. Not (the path) of those upon whom Thy wrath is brought down, nor of those who go astray.

10.12   Abraham

In the name of Allah, the Beneficent, the Merciful.
Alif Lam Ra. (This is) a Book which We have revealed to you that you may bring forth men, by their Lord's permission from utter darkness into light— to the way of the Mighty, the Praised One,
(Of) Allah, Whose is whatever is in the heavens and whatever Is in the earth; and woe to the unbelievers on account of the severe chastisement,
(To) those who love this world's life more than the hereafter, and turn away from Allah's path and desire to make it crooked; these are in a great error.
And We did not send any apostle but with the language of his people, so that he might explain to them clearly; then Allah makes whom He pleases err and He guides whom He pleases and He is the Mighty, the Wise.
And certainly We sent Musa with Our communications, saying: Bring forth your people from utter darkness into light and remind them of the days of Allah; most surely there are signs in this for every patient, grateful one.

And when Musa said to his people: Call to mind Allah's favor to you when He delivered you from Firon's people, who subjected you to severe torment, and slew your sons and spared your women; and in this there was a great trial from your Lord.

And when your Lord made it known: If you are grateful, I would certainly give to you more, and if you are ungrateful, My chastisement is truly severe.

And Musa said: If you are ungrateful, you and those on earth all together, most surely Allah is Self-sufficient, Praised;

Has not the account reached you of those before you, of the people of Nuh and Ad and Samood, and those after them? None knows them but Allah. Their apostles come to them with clear arguments, but they thrust their hands into their mouths and said: Surely we deny that with which you are sent, and most surely we are in serious doubt as to that to which you invite us.

Their apostles said: Is there doubt about Allah, the Maker of the heavens and the earth? He invites you to forgive you your faults and to respite you till an appointed term. They said: You are nothing but mortals like us; you wish to turn us away from what our fathers used to worship; bring us therefore some clear authority.

Their apostles said to them: We are nothing but mortals like yourselves, but Allah bestows (His) favors on whom He pleases of His servants, and it is not for us that we should bring you an authority except by Allah's permission; and on Allah should the believers rely.

And what reason have we that we should not rely on Allah? And He has indeed guided us in our ways; and certainly we would bear with patience your persecution of us; and on Allah should the reliant rely.

And those who disbelieved said to their apostles: We will most certainly drive you forth from our land, or else you shall come back into our religion. So their Lord revealed to them: Most certainly We will destroy the unjust.

And most certainly We will settle you in the land after them; this is for him who fears standing in My presence and who fears My threat.

And they asked for judgment and every insolent opposer was disappointed:

Hell is before him and he shall be given to drink of festering water:

He will drink it little by little and will not be able to swallow it agreeably, and death will come to him from every quarter, but he shall not die; and there shall be vehement chastisement before him.

The parable of those who disbelieve in their Lord: their actions are like ashes on which the wind blows hard on a stormy day; they shall not have power over any thing out of what they have earned; this is the great error.

Do you not see that Allah created the heavens and the earth with truth? If He please He will take you off and bring a new creation,

And this is not difficult for Allah.

And they shall all come forth before Allah, then the weak shall say to those who were proud: Surely we were your followers, can you therefore avert from us any part of the chastisement of Allah? They would say: If Allah had guided us, we too would have guided you; it is the same to us whether we are impatient (now) or patient, there is no place for us to fly to.

And the Shaitan shall say after the affair is decided: Surely Allah promised you the promise of truth, and I gave you promises, then failed to keep them to you, and I had no authority over you, except that I called you and you obeyed me, therefore do not blame me but blame yourselves: I cannot be your aider (now) nor can you be my aiders; surely I disbelieved in your associating me with Allah before; surely it is the unjust that shall have the painful punishment.

And those who believe and do good are made to enter gardens, beneath which rivers flow, to abide in them by their Lord's permission; their greeting therein is, Peace.

Have you not considered how Allah sets forth a parable of a good word (being) like a good tree, whose root is firm and whose branches are in heaven,

Yielding its fruit in every season by the permission of its Lord? And Allah sets forth parables for men that they may be mindful.

And the parable of an evil word is as an evil tree pulled up from the earth's surface; it has no stability.

Allah confirms those who believe with the sure word in this world's life and in the hereafter, and Allah causes the unjust to go astray, and Allah does what He pleases.

Have you not seen those who have changed Allah's favor for ungratefulness and made their people to alight into the abode of perdition

(Into hell? They shall enter into it and an evil place it is to settle in.

And they set up equals with Allah that they may lead (people) astray from His path. Say: Enjoy yourselves, for surely your return is to the fire.

Say to My servants who believe that they should keep up prayer and spend out of what We have given them secretly and openly before the coming of the day in which there shall be no bartering nor mutual befriending.

Allah is He Who created the heavens and the earth and sent down water from the clouds, then brought forth with it fruits as a sustenance for you, and He has made the ships subservient to you, that they might run their course in the sea by His command, and He has made the rivers subservient to you.

And He has made subservient to you the sun and the moon pursuing their courses, and He has made subservient to you the night and the day.

And He gives you of all that you ask Him; and if you count Allah's favors, you will not be able to number them; most surely man is very unjust, very ungrateful.

And when Ibrahim said: My Lord! make this city secure, and save me and my sons from worshipping idols:

My Lord! surely they have led many men astray; then whoever follows me, he is surely of me, and whoever disobeys me, Thou surely arc Forgiving, Merciful:

O our Lord! surely I have settled a part of my offspring in a valley unproductive of fruit near Thy Sacred House, our Lord! that they may keep up prayer; therefore make the hearts of some people yearn towards them and provide them with fruits; haply they may be grateful.

10.13 Al-Hijr

In the name of Allah, the Beneficent, the Merciful.

Alif Lam Ra. These are the verses of the Book and (of) a Quran that makes (things) clear.

Often will those who disbelieve wish that they had been Muslims.

Leave them that they may eat and enjoy themselves and (that) hope may beguile them, for they will soon know.

And never did We destroy a town but it had a term made known.

No people can hasten on their doom nor can they postpone (it).

And they say: O you to whom the Reminder has been revealed! you are most surely insane:

Why do you not bring to us the angels if you are of the truthful ones?

We do not send the angels but with truth, and then they would not be respited.

Surely We have revealed the Reminder and We will most surely be its guardian.

And certainly We sent (apostles) before you among the nations of yore.

And there never came an apostle to them but they mocked him.

Thus do We make it to enter into the hearts of the guilty;

They do not believe in it, and indeed the example of the former people has already passed.

And even if We open to them a gateway of heaven, so that they ascend into it all the while,

They would certainly say: Only our eyes.have been covered over, rather we are an enchanted people.

And certainly We have made strongholds in the heaven and We have made it fair seeming to the beholders.

And We guard it against every accursed Shaitan,

 But he who steals a hearing, so there follows him a visible flame.

And the earth—We have spread it forth and made in it firm mountains and caused to grow in it of every suitable thing.

And We have made in it means of subsistence for you and for him for whom you are not the suppliers.

And there is not a thing but with Us are the treasures of it, and We do not send it down but in a known measure.

And We send the winds fertilizing, then send down water from the cloud so We give it to you to drink of, nor is it you who store it up.

And most surely We bring to life and cause to die and We are the heirs.

 And certainly We know those of you who have gone before and We certainly know those who shall come later.

 And surely your Lord will gather them together; surely He is Wise, Knowing.

 And certainly We created man of clay that gives forth sound, of black mud fashioned in shape.

And the jinn We created before, of intensely hot fire.

And when your Lord said to the angels: Surely I am going to create a mortal of the essence of black mud fashioned in shape.

So when I have made him complete and breathed into him of My spirit, fall down making obeisance to him.

So the angels made obeisance, all of them together,

But Iblis (did it not); he refused to be with those who made obeisance.

He said: O Iblis! what excuse have you that you are not with those who make obeisance?

He said: I am not such that I should make obeisance to a mortal whom Thou hast created of the essence of black mud fashioned in shape.

He said: Then get out of it, for surely you are driven away:

And surely on you is curse until the day of judgment.

He said: My Lord! then respite me till the time when they are raised.

He said: So surely you are of the respited ones

Till the period of the time made known.

He said: My Lord! because Thou hast made life evil to me, I will certainly make (evil) fair-seeming to them on earth, and I will certainly cause them all to deviate

Except Thy servants from among them, the devoted ones.

He said: This is a right way with Me:

Surely. as regards My servants, you have no authority ,over them except those who follow you of the deviators.

And surely Hell is the promised place of them all:

It has seven gates; for every gate there shall be a separate party of them.

Surely those who guard (against evil) shall be in the midst of gardens and fountains:
 Enter them in peace, secure.

And We will root out whatever of rancor is in their breasts— (they shall be) as brethren, on raised couches, face to face.

Toil shall not afflict them in it, nor shall they be ever ejected from it.

Inform My servants that I am the Forgiving, the Merciful,

And that My punishment— that is the painful punishment.

And inform them of the guests of Ibrahim:

When they entered upon him, they said, Peace. He said: Surely we are afraid of you.

They said: Be not afraid, surely we give you the good news of a boy, possessing knowledge.

He said: Do you give me good news (of a son) when old age has come upon me?— Of what then do you give me good news!

They said: We give you good news with truth, therefore be not of the despairing.

He said: And who despairs of the mercy of his Lord but the erring ones?

He said: What is your business then, O messengers?

They said: Surely we are sent towards a guilty people,

Except Lut's followers: We will most surely deliver them all,

Except his wife; We ordained that she shall surely be of those who remain behind.

So when the messengers came to Lut's followers,

He said: Surely you are an unknown people.

They said: Nay, we have come to you with that about which they disputed.

And we have come to you with the truth, and we are most surely truthful.

Therefore go forth with your followers in a part of the night and yourself follow their rear, and let not any one of you turn round, and go forth whither you are commanded.

And We revealed to him this decree, that the roots of these shall be cut off in the morning.

And the people of the town came rejoicing.

He said: Surely these are my guests, therefore do not disgrace me,

And guard against (the punishment of) Allah and do not put me to shame.

They said: Have we not forbidden you from (other) people?

He said: These are my daughters, if you will do (aught).

By your life! they were blindly wandering on in their intoxication.

So the rumbling overtook them (while) entering upon the time of sunrise;

Thus did We turn it upside down, and rained down upon them stones of what had been decreed.

Surely in this are signs for those who examine.

And surely it is on a road that still abides.

Most surely there is a sign in this for the believers.

And the dwellers of the thicket also were most surely unjust.

So We inflicted retribution on them, and they are both, indeed, on an open road (still) pursued.

And the dwellers of the Rock certainly rejected the messengers;

And We gave them Our communications, but they turned aside from them;

And they hewed houses in the mountains in security.

So the rumbling overtook them in the morning;

And what they earned did not avail them.

And We did not create the heavens and the earth and what is between them two but in truth; and the hour is most surely coming, so turn away with kindly forgiveness.

Surely your Lord is the Creator of all things, the Knowing.

And certainly We have given you seven of the oft-repeated (verses) and the grand Quran.

Do not strain your eyes after what We have given certain classes of them to enjoy, and do not grieve for them, and make yourself gentle to the believers.

And say: Surely I am the plain warner.

Like as We sent down on the dividers

Those who made the Quran into shreds.

So, by your Lord, We would most certainly question them all,

 As to what they did.

Therefore declare openly what you are bidden and turn aside from the polytheists.

Surely We will suffice you against the scoffers

Those who set up another god with Allah; so they shall soon know.

And surely We know that your breast straitens at what they say;

Therefore celebrate the praise of your Lord, and be of those who make And serve your Lord until there comes to you that which is certain.

10.14   Light

In the name of Allah, the Beneficent, the Merciful.

(This is) a chapter which We have revealed and made obligatory and in which We have revealed clear communications that you may be mindful.

(As for) the fornicatress and the fornicator, flog each of them, (giving) a hundred stripes, and let not pity for them detain you in the matter of obedience to Allah, if you believe in Allah and the last day, and let a party of believers witness their chastisement.

The fornicator shall not marry any but a fornicatress or idolatress, and (as for) the fornicatress, none shall marry her but a fornicator or an idolater; and it is forbidden to the believers.

And those who accuse free women then do not bring four witnesses, flog them, (giving) eighty stripes, and do not admit any evidence from them ever; and these it is that are the transgressors,

Except those who repent after this and act aright, for surely Allah is Forgiving, Merciful.

And (as for) those who accuse their wives and have no witnesses except themselves, the evidence of one of these (should be taken) four times, bearing Allah to witness that he is most surely of the truthful ones.

And the fifth (time) that the curse of Allah be on him if he is one of the liars.

And it shall avert the chastisement from her if she testify four times, bearing Allah to witness that he is most surely one of the liars;

And the fifth (time) that the wrath of Allah be on her if he is one of the truthful.

And were it not for Allah's grace upon you and His mercy— and that Allah is Oft-returning (to mercy), Wise!

Surely they who concocted the lie are a party from among you. Do not regard it an evil to you; nay, it is good for you. Every man of them shall have what he has earned of sin; and (as for) him who took upon himself the main part thereof, he shall have a grievous chastisement.

Why did not the believing men and the believing women, when you heard it, think well of their own people, and say: This is an evident falsehood?

Why did they not bring four witnesses of it? But as they have not brought witnesses they are liars before Allah.

And were it not for Allah's grace upon you and His mercy in this world and the hereafter, a grievous chastisement would certainly have touched you on account of the discourse which you entered into.

When you received it with your tongues and spoke with your mouths what you had no knowledge of, and you deemed it an easy matter while with Allah it was grievous.

And why did you not, when you heard it, say: It does not beseem us that we should talk of it; glory be to Thee! this is a great calumny?

Allah admonishes you that you should not return to the like of it ever again if you are believers.

And Allah makes clear to you the communications; and Allah is Knowing, Wise.

Surely (as for) those who love that scandal should circulate respecting those who believe, they shall have a grievous chastisement in this world and the hereafter; and Allah knows, while you do not know.

And were it not for Allah's grace on you and His mercy, and that Allah is Compassionate, Merciful.

O you who believe! do not follow the footsteps of the Shaitan, and whoever follows the footsteps of the Shaitan, then surely he bids the doing of indecency and evil; and were it not for Allah's grace upon you and His mercy, not one of you would have ever been pure, but Allah purifies whom He pleases; and Allah is Hearing, Knowing.

And let not those of you who possess grace and abundance swear against giving to the near of kin and the poor and those who have fled in Allah's way, and they should pardon and turn away. Do you not love that Allah should forgive you? And Allah is Forgiving, Merciful.

Surely those who accuse chaste believing women, unaware (of the evil), are cursed in this world and the hereafter, and they shall have a grievous chastisement.

On the day when their tongues and their hands and their feet shall bear witness against them as to what they did.

On that day Allah will pay back to them in full their just reward, and they shall know that Allah is the evident Truth.

Bad women .are for bad men and bad men are for bad women. Good women are for good men and good men are for good women

O you who believe! Do not enter houses other than your own houses until you have asked permission and saluted their inmates; this is better for you, that you may be mindful.

But if you do not find any one therein, then do not enter them until permission is given to you; and if it is said to you: Go back, then go back; this is purer for you; and Allah is Cognizant of what you do.

It is no sin in you that you enter uninhabited houses wherein you have your necessaries; and Allah knows what you do openly and what you hide.

Say to the believing men that they cast down their looks and guard their private parts; that is purer for them; surely Allah is Aware of what they do.

And say to the believing women that they cast down their looks and guard their private parts and do not display their ornaments except what appears thereof, and let them wear their head-coverings over their bosoms, and not display their ornaments except to their husbands or their fathers, or the fathers of their husbands, or their sons, or the sons of their husbands, or their brothers, or their brothers' sons, or their sisters' sons, or their women, or those whom their right hands possess, or the male servants not having need (of women), or the children who have not attained knowledge of what is hidden of women; and let them not strike their feet so that what they hide of their ornaments may be known; and turn to Allah all of you, O believers! so that you may be successful.

And marry those among you who are single and those who are fit among your male slaves and your female slaves; if they are needy, Allah will make them free from want out of His grace; and Allah is Ample-giving, Knowing.

And let those who do not find the means to marry keep chaste until Allah makes them free from want out of His grace. And (as for) those who ask for a writing from among those whom your right hands possess, give them the writing if you know any good in them, and give them of the wealth of Allah which He has given you; and do not compel your slave girls to prostitution, when they desire to keep chaste, in order to seek the frail good of this world's life; and whoever compels them, then surely after their compulsion Allah is Forgiving, Merciful.

And certainly We have sent to you clear communications and a description of those who have passed away before you, and an admonition to those who guard (against evil).

Allah is the light of the heavens and the earth; a likeness of His light is as a niche in which is a lamp, the lamp is in a glass, (and) the glass is as it were a brightly shining star, lit from a blessed olive-tree, neither eastern nor western, the oil whereof almost gives light though fire touch it not— light upon light— Allah guides to His light whom He pleases, and Allah sets forth parables for men, and Allah is Cognizant of all things.

In houses which Allah has permitted to be exalted and that His name may be remembered in them; there glorify Him therein in the mornings and the evenings,

Men whom neither merchandise nor selling diverts from the remembrance of Allah and the keeping up of prayer and the giving of poor-rate; they fear a day in which the hearts and eyes shall turn about;

That Allah may give them the best reward of what they have done, and give them more out of His grace; and Allah gives sustenance to whom He pleases without measure.

And (as for) those who disbelieve, their deeds are like the mirage in a desert, which the thirsty man deems to be water; until when he comes to it he finds it to be naught, and there he finds Allah, so He pays back to him his reckoning in full; and Allah is quick in reckoning;

Or like utter darkness in the deep sea: there covers it a wave above which is another wave, above which is a cloud, (layers of) utter darkness one above another; when he holds out his hand, he is almost unable to see it; and to whomsoever Allah does not give light, he has no light.

Do you not see that Allah is He Whom do glorify all those who are in the heavens and the earth, and the (very) birds with expanded wings? He knows the prayer of each one and its glorification, and Allah is Cognizant of what they do.

And Allah's is the kingdom of the heavens and the earth, and to Allah is the eventual coming.

Do you not see that Allah drives along the clouds, then gathers them together, then piles them up, so that you see the rain coming forth from their midst? And He sends down of the clouds that are (like) mountains wherein is hail, afflicting therewith whom He pleases and turning it away from whom He pleases; the flash of His lightning almost takes away the sight.

Allah turns over the night and the day; most surely there is a lesson in this for those who have sight.

And Allah has created from water every living creature: so of them is that which walks upon its belly, and of them is that which walks upon two feet, and of them is that which walks upon four; Allah creates what He pleases; surely Allah has power over all things.

Certainly We have revealed clear communications, and Allah guides whom He pleases to the right way.

And they say: We believe in Allah and in the apostle and we obey; then a party of them turn back after this, and these are not believers.

And when they are called to Allah and His Apostle that he may judge between them, lo! a party of them turn aside.

And if the truth be on their side, they come to him quickly, obedient.

Is there in their hearts a disease, or are they in doubt, or do they fear that Allah and His Apostle will act wrongfully towards them? Nay! they themselves are the unjust.

The response of the believers, when they are invited to Allah and His Apostle that he may judge between them, is only to say: We hear and we obey; and these it is that are the successful.

And he who obeys Allah and His Apostle, and fears Allah, and is careful of (his duty to) Him, these it is that are the achievers.

And they swear by Allah with the most energetic of their oaths that if you command them they would certainly go forth. Say: Swear not; reasonable obedience (is desired); surely Allah is aware of what you do.

Say: Obey Allah and obey the Apostle; but if you turn back, then on him rests that which is imposed on him and on you rests that which is imposed on you; and if you obey him, you are on the right way; and nothing rests on the Apostle but clear delivering (of the message).

Allah has promised to those of you who believe and do good that He will most certainly make them rulers in the earth as He made rulers those before them, and that He will most certainly establish for them their religion which He has chosen for them, and that He will most certainly, after their fear, give them security in exchange; they shall serve Me, not associating aught with Me; and whoever is ungrateful after this, these it is who are the. transgressors.

And keep up prayer and pay the poor-rate and obey the Apostle, so that mercy may be shown to you.

Think not that those who disbelieve shall escape in the earth, and their abode is the fire; and certainly evil is the resort!

O you who believe! let those whom your right hands possess and those of you who have not attained to puberty ask permission of you three times; before the morning prayer, and when you put off your clothes at midday in summer, and after the prayer of the nightfall; these are three times of privacy for you; neither is it a sin for you nor for them besides these, some of you must go round about (waiting) upon others; thus does Allah make clear to you the communications, and Allah is Knowing, Wise.

And when the children among you have attained to puberty, let them seek permission as those before them sought permission; thus does Allah make clear to you His communications, and Allah is knowing, Wise.

And (as for) women advanced in years who do not hope for a marriage, it is no sin for them if they put off their clothes without displaying their ornaments; and if they restrain themselves it is better for them; and Allah is Hearing, Knowing.

There is no blame on the blind man, nor is there blame on the lame, nor is there blame on the sick, nor on yourselves that you eat from your houses, or your fathers' houses or your mothers' houses, or your brothers' houses, or your sisters' houses, or your paternal uncles' houses, or your paternal aunts' houses, or your maternal uncles' houses, or your maternal aunts' houses, or what you possess the keys of, or your friends' (houses). It is no sin in you that you eat together or separately. So when you enter houses, greet your people with a salutation from Allah, blessed (and) goodly; thus does Allah make clear to you the communications that you may understand.

Only those are believers who believe in Allah and His Apostle, and when they are with him on a momentous affair they go not away until they have asked his permission; surely they who ask your permission are they who believe in Allah and His Apostle; so when they ask your permission for some affair of theirs, give permission to whom you please of them and ask forgiveness for them from Allah; surely Allah is Forgiving, Merciful.

Do not hold the Apostle's calling (you) among you to be like your calling one to the other; Allah indeed knows those who steal away from among you, concealing themselves; therefore let those beware who go against his order lest a trial afflict them or there befall them a painful chastisement.

Now surely Allah's is whatever is in the heavens and the earth; He knows indeed that to which you are conforming yourselves; and on the day on which they are returned to Him He will inform them of what they did; and Allah is Cognizant of all things.

These are from an electronic version of The Holy Qur'an, translated by M.H. Shakir and published by Tahrike Tarsile Qur'an, Inc.,
http://www.hti.umich.edu/k/koran/

10.3 Selections from *The Alchemy of Happiness*

Knowledge of self is the key to the knowledge of God, according to the saying: "He who knows himself knows God,"[1] and, as it is Written in the Koran, "We will show them Our signs in the world and *in themselves*, that the truth may be manifest to them." Now nothing is nearer to thee than thyself, and if thou knowest not thyself how canst thou know anything else? If thou sayest "I know myself," meaning thy outward shape, body, face, limbs, and so forth, such knowledge can never be a key to the knowledge of God. Nor, if thy knowledge as to that which is within only extends so far, that when thou art hungry thou eatest, and when thou art angry thou attackest some one, wilt thou progress any further in this path, for the beasts are thy partners in this? But real self-knowledge consists in knowing the following things: What art thou in thyself, and from whence hast thou come? Whither art thou going, and for what purpose hast thou come to tarry here awhile, and in what does thy real happiness and misery consist? Some of thy attributes are those of animals, some of devils, and some of angels, and thou hast to find out which of these attributes are accidental and which essential. Till thou knowest this, thou canst not find out where thy real happiness lies. The occupation of animals is eating, sleeping, and fighting; therefore, if thou art an animal, busy thyself in these things. Devils are busy in stirring up mischief, and in guile and deceit; if thou belongest to them, do their work. Angels contemplate the beauty of God, and are entirely free from animal qualities; if thou art of angelic nature, then strive towards thine origin, that thou mayest know and contemplate the Most High, and be delivered from the thraldom of lust and anger. Thou shouldest also discover why thou hast been created with these two animal instincts: whether that they should subdue and lead thee captive, or whether that thou shouldest subdue them, and, in thy upward progress, make of one thy steed and of the other thy weapon.

The first step to self-knowledge is to know that thou art composed of an outward shape, called the body, and an inward entity called the heart, or soul. By "heart" I do not mean the piece of flesh situated in the left of our bodies, but that which uses all the other faculties as its instruments and servants. In truth it does not belong to the visible world, but to the invisible, and has come into this world as a traveller visits a foreign country for the sake of merchandise, and will presently return to its native land. It is the knowledge of this entity and its attributes which is the key to the knowledge of God.

Some idea of the reality of the heart, or spirit, may be obtained by a man closing his eyes and forgetting everything around except his individuality. He will thus also obtain a glimpse of the unending nature of that individuality. Too close inquiry, however, into the essence of spirit is forbidden by the Law. In the Koran it is written: "They will question thee concerning the spirit. Say: 'The Spirit comes by the command of my Lord.'" Thus much is known of it that it is an indivisible essence belonging to the world of decrees, and that it is not from everlasting, but created. An exact philosophical knowledge of the spirit is not a necessary preliminary to walking in the path of religion, but comes rather as the result of self-discipline and perseverance in that path, as it is said in the Koran: "Those who strive in Our way, verily We will guide them to the right paths."

For the carrying on of this spiritual warfare by which the knowledge of oneself and of God is to be obtained, the body may be figured as a kingdom, the soul as its king, and the different senses and faculties as constituting an army. Reason may be called the vizier, or prime minister, passion the revenue-collector, and anger the police-officer. Under the guise of collecting revenue, passion is continually prone to plunder on its own account, while resentment is always inclined to harshness and extreme severity. Both of these, the revenue-collector and the police-officer, have to be kept in due subordination to the king, but not killed or expelled, as they have their own proper functions to fulfil. But if passion and resentment master reason, the ruin of the soul infallibly ensues. A soul which allows its lower faculties to dominate the higher is as one who should hand over an angel to the power of a dog or a Mussalman to the tyranny of an unbeliever. The cultivation of demonic, animal, or angelic qualities results in the production of corresponding characters, which in the Day of Judgment will be manifested in visible shapes, the sensual appearing as swine, the ferocious as dogs and wolves, and the pure as angels. The aim of moral discipline is to purify the heart from the rust of passion and resentment, till, like a clear mirror, it reflects the light of God.

Some one may here object, "But if man has been created with animal and demonic qualities as well as angelic, how are we to know that the latter constitute his real essence, while the former are merely accidental and transitory?" To this I answer that the essence of each creature is to be sought in that which is highest in it and peculiar to it. Thus the horse and the ass are both burden-bearing animals, but the superiority of the horse to the ass consists in its being adapted for use in battle. If it fails in this, it becomes degraded to the rank of burden-bearing animals. Similarly with man: the highest faculty in him is reason, which fits him for the contemplation of God. If this. predominates in him, when he dies, he leaves behind him all tendencies to passion and resentment, and becomes capable of association with angels. As regards his mere animal qualities, man is inferior to many animals, but reason makes him superior to them, as it is written in the Koran: "To man We have subjected all things in the earth." But if his lower tendencies have triumphed, after death he will ever be looking towards the earth and longing for earthly delights.

Now the rational soul in man abounds in, marvels, both of knowledge and power. By means of it he masters arts and sciences, can pass in a flash from earth to heaven and back again, can map out the skies and measure the distances between the stars. By it also he can draw the fish from the sea and the birds from the air, and can subdue to his service animals, like the elephant, the camel, and the horse. His five senses are like five doors opening on the external world; but, more wonderful than this, his heart has a window which opens on the unseen world of spirits. In the state of sleep, when the avenues of the senses are closed, this window is opened and man receives impressions from the unseen world and sometimes foreshadowings of the future. His heart is then like a mirror which reflects what is pictured in the Tablet of Fate. But, even in sleep, thoughts of worldly things dull this mirror, so, that the impressions it receives are not clear. After death, however, such thoughts vanish and things are seen in their naked reality, and the saying in the Koran is fulfilled: "We have stripped the veil from off thee and thy sight today is keen."

This opening of a window in the heart towards the unseen also takes place in conditions. approaching those of prophetic inspiration, when intuitions spring up in the mind unconveyed through any sense-channel. The more a man purifies himself from fleshly lusts and concentrates his mind on God, the more conscious will he be of such intuitions. Those who are not conscious of them have no right to deny their reality. Nor are such intuitions confined only to those of prophetic rank. Just as iron, by sufficient polishing, can be made into a mirror, so any mind by due discipline can be rendered receptive of such impressions. It was at this truth the Prophet hinted when he said, "Every child is born with a predisposition towards Islam; then his parents make a Jew, or a, Christian, or a star-worshipper of him." Every human being has in the depths of his consciousness heard the question "Am I not your Lord?" and answered "Yes" to it. But some hearts are like mirrors so befouled with rust and dirt that they give no clear reflections, while those of the prophets and saints, though they are men "of like passions with us," are extremely sensitive to all divine impressions.

Nor is it only by reason of knowledge acquired and intuitive that the soul of man holds the first rank among created things, but also by reason of power. Just as angels preside over the elements, so does the soul rule the members of the body. Those souls which attain a special degree of power not only rule their own body but those of others also. If they wish a sick man to recover he recovers, or a person in health to fall ill he becomes ill, or if they will the presence of a person he comes to them. According as the effects produced by these powerful souls are good or bad they are termed miracles or sorceries. These souls differ from common folk in three ways: (1) what others only see in dreams they see in their waking moments. (2) While others' wills only affect their own bodies, these, by will-power, can move bodies extraneous to themselves. (3) The knowledge which others acquire by laborious learning comes to them by intuition.

These three, of course, are not the only marks which differentiate them from common people, but the only ones that come within our cognisance. Just as no one knows the real nature of God but God Himself, so no one knows the real nature of a prophet but a prophet. Nor is this to be wondered at, as in everyday matters we see that it is impossible to explain the charm of poetry to one whose ear is insusceptible of cadence and rhythm, or the glories of colour to one who is stone-blind. Besides mere incapacity, there are other hindrances to the attainment of spiritual truth. One of these is externally acquired knowledge. To use a figure, the heart may be represented as a well, and the five senses as five streams which are continually conveying water to it. In order to find out the real contents of the heart these streams must be stopped for a time, at any rate, and the refuse they have brought with them must be cleared out of the well. In other words, if we are to arrive at pure spiritual truth, we must put away, for the time, knowledge which has been acquired by, external processes and which too often hardens into dogmatic prejudice.

A mistake of an opposite kind is made by shallow people who, echoing some phrases which they have caught from Sufi teachers, go about decrying all knowledge. This is as if a person who was not an adept in alchemy were to go about saying, "Alchemy is better than in gold," and were to refuse gold when it was offered to him. Alchemy is better than gold, but real alchemists are very rare, and so are real Sufis. He who has a mere smattering of Sufism is not superior to a learned main, any more than he who has tried a few experiments in alchemy has ground for despising a rich man.

Any one who will look into the matter will see that happiness is necessarily linked with the knowledge of God. Each faculty of ours delights in that for which it was created: lust delights in accomplishing desire, anger in taking vengeance, the eye in seeing beautiful objects, and the ear in hearing harmonious sounds. The highest function of the soul of man is the perception of truth; in this accordingly it finds its special delight. Even in trifling matters, such, as learning chess, this holds good, and the higher the subject-matter of the knowledge obtained the greater the delight. A man would be pleased at being admitted into the confidence of a prime minister, but how much more if the king makes an intimate of him and discloses state secrets to him!

An astronomer who, by his knowledge, can map the stars and describe their courses, derives more pleasure from his knowledge than the chess-player from his. Seeing, then, that nothing is higher than God, how great must be the delight which springs from the true knowledge of Him!

THE ALCHEMY OF HAPPINESS BY AL GHAZZALI
CLAUD FIELD, translator [b. 1863, d. 1941] [1909]
http://www.sacred-texts.com/isl/tah/tah05.htm

10.4   Selections from the Mystical Poetry of Rumi.

People claim that there exists in the human soul a kind of depravity you do not find in animals or wild beasts. Since men do not practice surrender and obedience to God they become inferior to the animals. God has said in the Koran of people like these: "They are real wild animals, and even more lost."

Bad character and depravity in man are a veil that hides his deep essence; these dark dispositions see to it that his essence is veiled, and this veil cannot be dissolved except through immense efforts. These efforts are of every kind. The greatest is to mingle with friends who have turned their face towards God and have turned away from this world. There is no combat harder for a human being than to associate himself with holy and pious people: seeing them annihilates and dissolves the carnal soul. They say, "When a serpent hasn't seen a man for forty years, it becomes a dragon; it becomes this because it hasn't met or seen that being that could be the cause of the dissolution of its perversity or of its evil character."

Wherever a strong lock is used, there is something extremely precious hidden. The thicker the veil, the more valuable the jewel. A hoard of treasure is guarded by a large snake; don't dwell on the hideousness of the snake, contemplate the dazzling and priceless things you'll discover in the treasure.

Biographer

Just wait for what'll happen when I vanish!
Those whose love warmed you will dig your tomb
And make you a food for ants and reptiles.
Those who often cane to you aflame with desire
Will stop up their noses at your stink."

epic

Rumi used to say again and again: "In the name of God, see to it that you pray constantly, so that your worldly means and heirs and friends become numerous; when the Resurrection comes, you will console your friends through these prayers. It is certain that, through the blessing that is attached to prayer, anyone who asks and begs will he granted their desires both on the Path and in the world."

It is also reported that when Rumi saw someone occupied assiduously in the accomplishment of the rites of canonical prayer, he would cry out: "Well done, servant full of zeal, humble and modest slave! That man is brave that cannot be shaken from the service of his master, and who practices his devotions for as long as lie has the strength."

Biographer

Only that being whose robe's torn by great passion
Is purified of greed and all its harm!
Blessing on you, Love, who bring us your gifts,
Who is the doctor for all our evils,
The cure for our pride and vanity, our Plato and Galen!
Through Love, our earthly body has flown to heaven,
The mountain began to dance and became agile.
Love inspired Mount Sinai, O lover! So Sinai
Grew drunk and Moses fell down, stricken with glory.
I also, like a pipe, can say anything at all
When I'm joined, in harmony, with my Friend:
Separate from the one who speaks, I grow silent, Even if I know a hundred songs.
When the rose has gone and the garden faded,
You won't hear any more of the nightingale's story.
The Beloved is all that lives, the lover a dead thing.

King, saint, thief, madman—
Love has grabbed everyone by the neck
And drags Lis to God by secret ways....
How could I ever have guessed
That God, too, desired us?

Sikhism

11.1 Selections from the Hymns of Guru Arjan

Saith Nanak, when the Bridegroom sitteth at home with me adorned are my beautiful gates;

The nine treasures in abundance then enter my house,

And I obtain everything, everything by meditating on the Name.

By meditation on the Name with composure and devotion God is ever my Helper.

My cares are at an end, my transmigration hath ceased, and my mind no longer feeleth anxiety.

When I call out God's name, spontaneous music playeth, and there is a scene of wondrous splendour.

Saith Nanak, when the Beloved is with me, I obtain the nine treasures.

All my brethren and friends became overjoyed

When I on meeting the Guru conquered in the very toilsome struggle of the arena;

When on meeting the Guru I repeated God's name, I conquered and the walls of the fortress of error were demolished.

I obtained the wealth of many treasures, and God stood by to assist me.

He whom God hath made His own possesseth divine knowledge, and is conspicuous among men.

Saith Nanak, the brethren and friends of him on whose side standeth God rejoice.

How man should love God:

When water and milk are placed over a fire, the water alloweth not the milk to burn; O men, in that way love God.

As the bumble-bee becometh entangled and intoxicated by the odour of the lotus, and leaveth it not even for a moment,

So relax not a whit thy love for God; dedicate to Him all thine ornaments and enjoyments.

Man in the company of the saints hath no fear of what is called the way of death where wailings are heard.

Sing and meditate on God's praises, and all thy sins and sorrows shall depart.

Saith Nanak, chant the song of God, O man, love Him and bear Him such affection in thy heart

As a fish beareth water; it hath not a moment's happiness out of it; such love bear God, O man.

The chatrik thirsty for raindrops chirrupeth every moment 'ain, beautiful cloud!'

So love God, give Him thy soul and fix all thine attention on Him.

Be not proud, seek God's protection, sacrifice thyself for a sight of Him.

The woman who hath true love for the Guru and with whom he is well pleased, shall meet her parted Spouse.

Saith Nanak, chant the song of the eternal God; love Him,

O my soul, and bear Him such affection

As the love of the sheldrake for the sun; she feeleth much anxiety as to when she shall behold the day.

As the kokil in love with the mango sweetly singeth, so love God, O man:

Love God, be not proud, all are but guests of a single night.

Now why art thou, who camest and shalt depart naked, attached to and enamoured of the world?

By entering the asylum of the feet of the pious, the worldly love thou feelest now shall depart, and stability be thine,

Saith Nanak, sing the chant of the Merciful Being, O man, and love God *as the shel- drake* watcheth for the day.

As the deer at night hearing the sound of the bell giveth its life; so, O man, bear love to God.

As a wife in love with her husband waiteth on her beloved; so give thy heart to thy Darling:

So give thy heart to thy Darling, enjoy Him, and thou shalt obtain all happiness and bliss.

My friend, my Beloved, we have met after a very long time, and I have clothed myself in red.

When the Guru became the mediator, I saw God with mine eyes; none appeareth to me like my Beloved.

Saith Nanak, chant the song of the compassionate and fascinating One; O man, grasp God's feet and such love bear thou Him.

The great God to whom all creation is subject cannot be obtained by idle pilgrimages and ablutions:-

Of roaming and searching from forest to forest and of many ablutions I have become very weary.

Nanak, when I met the holy man, I found God in my heart,

Whom countless munis and penitents seek for,

Whom millions of Brahmas worship, and whose name is uttered by men of divine
    knowledge;
To meet whom, the Bright One, men perform devotion, penance, mortification, reli-
    gious ceremonies, worship, many purifications and adorations,
Wander over the earth, and bathe at places of pilgrimage.
O God, men, forests, glades, beasts, and birds all worship Thee.
The merciful beloved God is found, O Nanak, and salvation obtained by meeting
    the society of the saints.
Millions of incarnations of Vishnu and of Shiv with the matted hair
Desire Thee, O merciful One; for Thee their souls and bodies feel endless longing.
The Lord is infinite and unapproachable, He is the all-ervading God and Master.
Demigods, Sidhs, the crowd of celestial singers meditate on Thee; the Yakshas and
    Kinars utter Thy praises.
Millions of Indars and various gods repeat Thy name, O Lord, and hail Thee.
Thou art the Patron of the patronless, saith Nanak; Thou art the compassionate;
    associate me with the saints that I may be saved.

New Religious Movements

12.1 Selections from the Kitab-I-Aqadas

The first duty prescribed by God for His servants is the recognition of Him Who is the Dayspring of His Revelation and the Fountain of His laws, Who representeth the Godhead in both the Kingdom of His Cause and the world of creation. Whoso achieveth this duty hath attained unto all good; and whoso is deprived thereof hath gone astray, though he be the author of every righteous deed. It behoveth every one who reacheth this most sublime station, this summit of transcendent glory, to observe every ordinance of Him Who is the Desire of the world. These twin duties are inseparable. Neither is acceptable without the other. Thus hath it been decreed by Him Who is the Source of Divine inspiration.

They whom God hath endued with insight will readily recognize that the precepts laid down by God constitute the highest means for the maintenance of order in the world and the security of its peoples. He that turneth away from them is accounted among the abject and foolish. We, verily, have commanded you to refuse the dictates of your evil passions and corrupt desires, and not to transgress the bounds which the Pen of the Most High hath fixed, for these are the breath of life unto all created things. The seas of Divine wisdom and Divine utterance have risen under the breath of the breeze of the All-Merciful. Hasten to drink your fill, O men of understanding! They that have violated the Covenant of God by breaking His commandments, and have turned back on their heels, these have erred grievously in the sight of God, the All-Possessing, the Most High.

O ye peoples of the world! Know assuredly that My commandments are the lamps of My loving providence among My servants, and the keys of My mercy for My creatures. Thus hath it been sent down from the heaven of the Will of your Lord, the Lord of Revelation. Were any man to taste the sweetness of the words which the lips of the All-Merciful have willed to utter, he would, though the treasures of the earth be in his possession, renounce them one and all, that he might vindicate the truth of even one of His commandments, shining above the Dayspring of His bountiful care and loving-kindness.

Say: From My laws the sweet-smelling savour of My garment can be smelled, and by their aid the standards of Victory will be planted upon the highest peaks. The Tongue of My power hath, from the heaven of My omnipotent glory, addressed to My creation these words: "Observe My commandments, for the love of My beauty." Happy is the lover that hath inhaled the divine fragrance of his Best-Beloved from these words, laden with the perfume of a grace which no tongue can describe. By My life! He who hath drunk the choice wine of fairness from the hands of My bountiful favour will circle around My commandments that shine above the Dayspring of My creation.

Think not that We have revealed unto you a mere code of laws. Nay, rather, We have unsealed the choice Wine with the fingers of might and power. To this beareth witness that which the Pen of Revelation hath revealed. Meditate upon this, O men of insight!

We have enjoined obligatory prayer upon you, with nine rak'ahs, to be offered at noon and in the morning and the evening unto God, the Revealer of Verses. We have relieved you of a greater number, as a command in the Book of God. He, verily, is the Ordainer, the Omnipotent, the Unrestrained. When ye desire to perform this prayer, turn ye towards the Court of My Most Holy Presence, this Hallowed Spot that God hath made the Centre round which circle the Concourse on High, and which He hath decreed to be the Point of Adoration for the denizens of the Cities of Eternity, and the Source of Command unto all that are in heaven and on earth; and when the Sun of Truth and Utterance shall set, turn your faces towards the Spot that We have ordained for you. He, verily, is Almighty and Omniscient.

Everything that is hath come to be through His irresistible decree. Whenever My laws appear like the sun in the heaven of Mine utterance, they must be faithfully obeyed by all, though My decree be such as to cause the heaven of every religion to be cleft asunder. He doeth what He pleaseth. He chooseth, and none may question His choice. Whatsoever He, the Well-Beloved, ordaineth, the same is, verily, beloved. To this He Who is the Lord of all creation beareth Me witness. Whoso hath inhaled the sweet fragrance of the All-Merciful, and recognized the Source of this utterance, will welcome with his own eyes the shafts of the enemy, that he may establish the truth of the laws of God amongst men. Well is it with him that hath turned thereunto, and apprehended the meaning of His decisive decree.

We have set forth the details of obligatory prayer in another Tablet. Blessed is he who observeth that whereunto he hath been bidden by Him Who ruleth over all mankind. In the Prayer for the Dead six specific passages have been sent down by God, the Revealer of Verses. Let one who is able to read recite that which hath been revealed to precede these passages; and as for him who is unable, God hath relieved him of this requirement. He, of a truth, is the Mighty, the Pardoner.

Hair doth not invalidate your prayer, nor aught from which the spirit hath departed, such as bones and the like. Ye are free to wear the fur of the sable as ye would that of the beaver, the squirrel, and other animals; the prohibition of its use hath stemmed, not from the Qur'an, but from the misconceptions of the divines. He, verily, is the All-Glorious, the All-Knowing.

We have commanded you to pray and fast from the beginning of maturity; this is ordained by God, your Lord and the Lord of your forefathers. He hath exempted from this those who are weak from illness or age, as a bounty from His Presence, and He is the Forgiving, the Generous. God hath granted you leave to prostrate yourselves on any surface that is clean, for We have removed in this regard the limitation that had been laid down in the Book; God, indeed, hath knowledge of that whereof ye know naught. Let him that findeth no water for ablution repeat five times the words "In the Name of God, the Most Pure, the Most Pure", and then proceed to his devotions. Such is the command of the Lord of all worlds. In regions where the days and nights grow long, let times of prayer be gauged by clocks and other instruments that mark the passage of the hours. He, verily, is the Expounder, the Wise.

We have absolved you from the requirement of performing the Prayer of the Signs. On the appearance of fearful natural events call ye to mind the might and majesty of your Lord, He Who heareth and seeth all, and say "Dominion is God's, the Lord of the seen and the unseen, the Lord of creation".

It hath been ordained that obligatory prayer is to be performed by each of you individually. Save in the Prayer for the Dead, the practice of congregational prayer hath been annulled. He, of a truth, is the Ordainer, the All-Wise.

God hath exempted women who are in their courses from obligatory prayer and fasting. Let them, instead, after performance of their ablutions, give praise unto God, repeating ninety-five times between the noon of one day and the next "Glorified be God, the Lord of Splendour and Beauty". Thus hath it been decreed in the Book, if ye be of them that comprehend.

When travelling, if ye should stop and rest in some safe spot, perform ye—men and women alike—a single prostration in place of each unsaid Obligatory Prayer, and while prostrating say "Glorified be God, the Lord of Might and Majesty, of Grace and Bounty". Whoso is unable to do this, let him say only "Glorified be God"; this shall assuredly suffice him. He is, of a truth, the all-sufficing, the ever-abiding, the forgiving, compassionate God. Upon completing your prostrations, seat yourselves cross-legged—men and women alike—and eighteen times repeat "Glorified be God, the Lord of the kingdoms of earth and heaven". Thus doth the Lord make plain the ways of truth and guidance, ways that lead to one way, which is this Straight Path. Render thanks unto God for this most gracious favour; offer praise unto Him for this bounty that hath encompassed the heavens and the earth; extol Him for this mercy that hath pervaded all creation.

Say: God hath made My hidden love the key to the Treasure; would that ye might perceive it! But for the key, the Treasure would to all eternity have remained concealed; would that ye might believe it! Say: This is the Source of Revelation, the Dawning-place of Splendour, Whose brightness hath illumined the horizons of the world. Would that ye might understand!

This is, verily, that fixed Decree through which every irrevocable decree hath been established.

the Kitab-I-Aqadas
http://www.sacred-texts.com/bhi/aqdas.htm

12.2   Selections from the Sedona Vortex Experience

INTRODUCTION

The word vortex comes from the Latin word "vertere" which means "to turn or whirl." The dictionary defines the word "vortex" as a form of fluid motion in which particles travel in a circular path around an axis.

Water going down a drain forms a whirlpool or fluid vortex. Larger whirlpools are seen in the ocean. There, a whirling mass of water forms a vacuum and draws anything in its path into the center of the whirlpool.

Air is another type of fluid motion that can create a vortex. We have all seen pictures of—if not experienced—the powerful eddies of air that create whirlwinds and tornadoes. A vortex can form behind any blunt object that has some fluid flowing over it. As examples, the wind blowing around a house or water flowing around a boulder, form vortices.

From these examples—whirlpool, whirlwind, tornado—we see that a vortex has a definite shape, form, pattern, power, energy, and force. A vortex is often seen as a spiraling cone or funnel shape of awesome energy.

The dictionary also says that "any activity, situation or state of affairs that resembles a whirl or eddy in its rushing, absorbing effect, irresistible and catastrophic power, etc." is also defined as a vortex.

"I sat down on a vortex and haven't been the same since," is a humorous statement often voiced by many Sedonans. Is Sedona a vortex of powerful energy?

Does Sedona have some absorbing, irresistible, and at times catastrophic power? Ask any resident. The stories are as many and as varied as the people who live here.

"I was driving across country, tired of the freeways and thought I'd take a short, scenic, side trip. I got off I-17, took 179 toward Sedona. When I saw Bell Rock I burst into tears. I pulled off the road, walked to the base of that great monolith, fell down, hugged the rocks, and kissed the earth. I knew I was home!"

"Everything kept coming up Sedona," another true story begins. "I'd never been to Sedona, but I kept hearing about it from family, friends, strangers, on the radio, and on T.V. Something kept ringing a bell inside me every time I heard the word Sedona. One day I picked up a magazine at the grocery check out counter, opened it, and there was an article on 'Sedona.' That's it, I thought. I've got to check that place out...that was ten years ago. I think that Sedona is actually checking me out."

"I had been unhappy to the point of illness for some time. I started seeing my Baptist minister for counseling. We would always start the session with a prayer and ask the Holy Spirit for guidance and healing. After about five sessions I began feeling that my problems and illness were caused by the stress of the big city. 'I think I need to move to the country,' I said one day. My minister closed his eyes in prayer and then burst out with: 'Yes, and Spirit is telling me where.' 'Tell me,' I begged. 'No, that's for you to find out.'

The next day in the midst of smog, honking, and bumper to bumper traffic on the L.A. freeway, I felt a deep inner peace. I looked up at the car in front of me and saw a 'Sedona' bumper-sticker. I had an incredible rush of energy and tears welled up in my eyes.
     'Sedona!' I said to my minister, that Sunday at church.
     'You're very intuitive.' he smiled back."

Each person that has come to this land has seen the canyon open into a lush green valley along the creek bed. We have watched the sculpted Red Rocks leap up before us in almost mystical form. We have witnessed the naked edges of sandstone and basalt bend and stand silhouetted against the changing skies. And each of us has felt the power, mystery, and magic of this land called Sedona.
     People of all ages and walks of life hear the call of the canyon and are drawn to Sedona by the magic that is here. Artists see the magic as beauty. Retired folks experience the magic as clean air, country living, good health-qualities of the good life. Spiritually-oriented people are drawn to Sedona like moths to a flame, without even knowing why they came. Many people have-had the experience of being "called" to Sedona without any awareness of the power, mystery, and magic that is here.
     Recently Dick Sutphen and Page Bryant have written about Sedona as one of the major power points on the planet. Planet Earth is a living, changing, evolving being, that has places of power on it, much like we have acupressure points on our bodies. The power points or vorticies on the planet are places where energy can be seen, felt, and experienced. Unusual phenomena often occur at these places.
     In our materialistic culture, if we cannot see a thing with our physical eyes, we tend to think it doesn't exist. Yet we can see that energy and matter embody both the dense structures of New York skyscrapers as well as the lighter structures of fog and mist.

A pot of homemade soup brewing in the kitchen can definitely be perceived by someone in another part of the house. But what of things that the physical senses cannot pick up-energies that reach beyond our five physical senses? These energies are real, too. We need to develop new ways of seeing, smelling, touching, sensing, etc. in order to experience not only the Sedona Vortex energies, but the energies of our own vast, multidimensional beingness as well.

NATURE'S DYNAMIC HEALING ENERGY

All of nature is available to us to help us clear, heal, and release old traumas, emotional scars, and habituated thought patterns. The key is being receptive to Nature's dynamic healing energy. The following series of exercises will assist you in opening up to the healing energies in Nature.

After centering and grounding, move into a posture of receiving. Find a comfortable place, sit down, place your hands palms up on your lap, and inhale deeply. Receive Nature's gift of fresh, healing air. Relax your shoulders, slowly shake or spiral out any held tension. Roll your head and neck from side to side. Then focus on one of the following areas: Sound, Temperature, or Color.

SOUND—Place the palms of your hands over your ears while breathing deeply. Allow the soft movement of your breath to rise up through your neck into your head and brain. Then remove your hands and begin to focus on the sounds that you hear. Let your consciousness extend into each different sound. Then become one with all the sounds. Feel the waves of sound energy, starting at your outer ears, flowing into your inner ears. Let the waves of energy blend into one pulsating movement.

Accept the sounds of Nature—the sounds outside of yourself—as background music for your own inner sound of silence. Breathe into that inner core of silence. Allow the sounds and the silence to become a spiraling vortex of energy that propels you into your Divinity.

Listen to the musical sound of the creek as the water goes bellowing, murmuring and tinkling over the rocks. Allow the sound to wash through your body and mind. Let the soft, soothing sound flow through your consciousness, carrying away any debris left there by emotional storms. You can use the sounds of the birds and/or the bees in a similar manner as the above exercises. You can also "pretend" that you are the water, the birds, bees, or the sound-maker and then allow that experience to carry you into an inseparable oneness with all of Nature's dynamic healing energy.

TEMPERATURE—Sitting or lying in a comfortable place, begin to feel the warmth of the sun on your body. Let the warmth of the sun radiate deep into your bones—into your very core. Allow the warm feeling to spread out over your entire body. Let the warmth and the light from the sun fill every cell, tissue and muscle of your body. Imagine yourself in the heart of the sun. Imagine the sun radiating in your heart center. Breathe deeply and experience your magnificence.

Feel the cool breeze on your skin. Notice its gentle caress. Let its formlessness dance across your physical form. Allow your consciousness to join the dancing breeze. Breathe with the breeze. Let yourself expand. Feel more space both within your physical form and within the formlessness of your conscious awareness. Notice the breeze dancing in the trees. Notice a similar dancing movement somewhere in your body. Let yourself feel kissed, caressed, and loved by the breeze. Let the feeling of love fill your body and being. Then, get up and dance!

THE FORM AND THE FORMLESS

The atmosphere, ethers, and air that we breathe are filled with the energies of life. Scientists call this vast fluid of cosmic soup "interplanetary plasma." The formless energies of this interplanetary plasma are called into form, action, and being every day, moment-to-moment by our very breath.

Breath is life, energy, movement. Through our breath, we are linked to every other living thing on the planet. Our breath is automatic; yet, it is the only unconscious function over which we can take immediate, conscious control. Thus, our breath serves as a bridge, carrying us from unconscious robot-like existence to beings of conscious awareness and then into masters of super-conscious abilities.

With deep, conscious inhalations we can begin to feel our held energies loosen, lift, and expand. As we breathe deeply, our energies become like a colorful bouquet of balloons—graceful, flexible and joyfully moving in the free flow of life and energy around them, all the while anchored to their source. Throughout times, cultures, and religions, breath has been linked to spirit and spiritual realms. We can re-establish this link to spirit, source, and oneness with our breath.